DANGEROUS DAYS

DANGEROUS
DAYS

A DIGGER'S
GREAT ESCAPE

ERNEST BROUGH

ERNEST BROUGH IS DONATING HIS EARNINGS
FROM THE SALE OF THIS BOOK TO PATIENT CARE
AND RESEARCH INTO ALZHEIMER'S AND DEMENTIA AT
ST VINCENT'S HOSPITAL, MELBOURNE.

HarperCollins*Publishers*

For practical reasons, we have used both imperial and metric scales for measurements, and both pounds, shillings and pence and decimal currency throughout, as applicable in the author's circumstances.

HarperCollins*Publishers*

First published in Australia in 2009
by HarperCollins*Publishers* Pty Limited
ABN 36 009 913 517
A member of the HarperCollins*Publishers* (Australia) Pty Limited Group
www.harpercollins.com.au

HarperCollins*Publishers*
25 Ryde Road, Pymble, Sydney, NSW 2073, Australia
31 View Road, Glenfield, Auckland 0627, New Zealand
1–A, Hamilton House, Connaught Place, New Delhi – 110 001, India
77–85 Fulham Palace Road, London W6 8JB, United Kingdom
2 Bloor Street East, 20th Floor, Toronto, Ontario M4W 1A8, Canada
10 East 53rd Street, New York, NY 10022, USA

National Library of Australia Cataloguing-in-Publication data:

Brough, Ernest, 1920–.
   Dangerous days: a digger's great escape / Ernest Brough.
   ISBN 978 07322 8734 4 (pbk.).
   Brough, Ernest, 1920–
   World War, 1939–1945—Personal narratives, Australian.
   World War, 1939–1945—Prisoners and prisons, German.
   World War, 1939–1945—Prisoners and prisons, Italian.
   Prisoner-of-war escapes—Austria.
   Soldiers—Australia—Biography.
940.548194.

Cover and internal design by Matt Stanton
Cover images: soldiers courtesy Keystone/Getty Images;
   portrait of Ernest Brough courtesy National Library of Australia;
   tank courtesy Australian War Memorial, Negative Number 024859
Maps by Demap Cartographic Design
Typeset in Perpetua 12/16 Matt Stanton
Printed and bound in Australia by Griffin Press
70gsm Bulky Book Ivory used by HarperCollins*Publishers* is natural, recyclable product made from wood grown in sustainable forests. The manufacturing process conform to the environmental regulations in the country of origin, New Zealand.

7 6 5 4 3 2 1   09 10 11 12 13

For my mother, Anne,
and my father,
Ernest James Brough

CONTENTS

TIME TO TELL

It's still dark, maybe it's half an hour or so before dawn. We're exhausted, the three of us, starving, and Eric is crook, but we've got to keep going, make as much ground as we can, before we have to find somewhere to hide again. What will be waiting for us when the sun cracks the sky? The Gestapo or the Ustashi? The bullet with my name on it? I can't think about that. My mind goes as numb as my frozen hands and feet. We've got to keep going ...

I wake up with the dawn light, in my home in Geelong, safe, sixty-five years away from that night on the run with Eric and Allan. The cat is curled up on the end of the bed, undisturbed. The adrenalin and anxiety are long gone, but the images are as clear in my mind as ever, not like a bad dream, but like a film, except that it really happened. All these years on, it still amazes me that I am alive. I'm eighty-eight. My godfather, I'm an old bloke! And I'm very happy to have reached this ripe old age. Plenty of times Ernie Brough could have lost his life, and it's only luck, life's lottery, that decided to keep me here.

It was one decision of mine in particular, which I made when I was nineteen, that put me in the midst of the worst the lottery has to offer. I joined up with the Second Australian Imperial Forces at the beginning of World War II.

To this day, I don't know how or why the bullet with my name on it missed me. Well, a couple of bullets didn't miss me, but they didn't kill me either, and some might say the one I copped in the backside was always coming to me. Maybe, as they say, fortune favours the brave; or maybe only the good die young. I don't know how I survived the things I did. Fighting at Tobruk, and El Alamein, rotting in a couple of prison camps — in Italy, then Austria — escaping with Allan Berry and Eric Batty through Slovenia and into Croatia, and through the cut-throat madness of the Yugoslav liberation war. Was that me? Did I do all those things? Yes. There's nothing wrong with my memory, and I remember those days in minute detail.

Was I a hero? No, not especially. There are a lot of heroes in war, and a lot of them don't get home to tell you all about it. Everyone's a hero, and no-one is. Half of my hometown football team came back as shadows of their former selves, or not at all. I did get home, and I was all right. But for thirty or forty years afterwards, I couldn't talk much about it. Once, I got myself so twisted up, I even thought I might have to shoot myself. That's not uncommon. It takes a long time to make sense of some things, and some things will never make sense.

But now I am an old bloke, I can say what I like. I can tell my truths as I remember them. War is a terrible thing, we all know that. If I knew how to stop such stupid, pointless destruction, I'd do it today. It might seem strange, then, for me to say that I don't regret that decision I made when I was nineteen. To say the least, I learned an awful lot.

And I'm here, still here, to tell you all about it.

I
DON'T GO TO WAR

When I was a kid, a photograph of Albert Jacka sat on the sideboard in the dining room of our house. Albert Jacka was a hero back then; the most celebrated Australian soldier. He'd won the Victoria Cross at Gallipoli, the highest military honour of the British Empire, and was the first Australian to be awarded it in the Great War — some said he'd deserved two. He was also my mother's cousin and the mayor of St Kilda. I never met him; he died, of his battle injuries, when I was eleven. I never got too close to his photograph either, because us kids weren't allowed near Mum's sideboard. It was where she kept her crystal glasses and ornaments and that sort of thing: *Do not touch!*

We lived in a town called Drouin, a small town, about sixty

Drouin 1927. Me on the far left, aged 7, with big sister Marjorie, 9, brother Alex, 12, and little sister Nancy Jane, 6.

miles from Melbourne, in the lush countryside of Gippsland — Mum, Dad, me, my older brother, Alexander, my older sister, Marjorie, and my younger sister, Nancy Jane. We had a good childhood. Dad was strict, but always fair. His name, like mine, was Ernest James Brough. He was a tough man — short and lightly built, but strong; he'd been a boxer as a young man. He was tough in the way he lived and tough on himself. Dad drove a truck for the local grocer, supplying the farms in the area with chaff, manure and superphosphate — heavy work.

Some of my earliest memories are of Alex and Marjorie and me riding to school on our horse, Carbine. It was about a three-mile ride, the three of us sitting on an old corn sack on Carbine's back, and it wasn't always easy for a little bloke. Once, while climbing the steep rise of Burgoynes Hill, I slipped right off the back of him, pulling Marjorie off with me. We had to dust ourselves down, climb onto a nearby fence and remount. But it was fun, too: all us kids who rode to school would go down to the creek below the horse paddock after the bell, and on hot days we'd go for a skinny-dip and swim among all the little minnows in the water, before the long ride back home again.

A few years after starting primary school, we moved houses, closer to school, and us kids would walk the journey, because Nancy was with us by that time and we couldn't fit four on a horse. Our new house was right by the railway line

The Brough kids with their trusty steed, Carbine, 1927.

and the trains from Melbourne came past our front gate. In the evenings, and especially during the holidays, I'd chase the trains, calling out: 'Paper!' And out would come copies of the *Truth*, *Smith's Weekly*, *The Age*, the *Sun*, the *Argus*. The passengers had read their papers by the time the train got to Drouin, and I'd go home every night with a bundle of them under my arm, all of them smelling of cigar smoke.

Apart from Mum's precious sideboard treasures, we didn't have much in the way of worldly goods. We had a six-valve radio for a while — it worked really well until lightning came down the aerial pole one night and blew all the valves. We didn't have an icebox, or a fridge; in fact, we didn't have electricity connected to the house. We had kerosene lamps and a Coolgardie meat safe outside under the tank stand that only kept the flies off the food, really. When you got your meat in the summer, you had to cook it straight away; there was no way to keep it. I remember my mum was always on the go, never still: cooking, cleaning, sewing, making preserves, every day and in all weathers. In the summer, when she was at the stove, or washing at the copper, I'd watch the little beads of perspiration on her forehead. When she shopped, she walked the mile and a half into town, and walked that shopping all the way back again. They say a woman's work is never done: that was my mum; she gave me my first lessons in what it means to work, to be busy doing something every moment of the day.

As a kid, I loved to be outside the most, out in the yard, in the garden, or catching rabbits. I'd sell those rabbits for sixpence each. It was while I was out setting traps one day that I saw Kingsford Smith fly over in his famous plane, the *Southern Cross*. He was making his own pocket money doing joyrides — known as 'barnstorming' then — for five shillings at a time, landing and taking off at Ellinbank, near Warragul, a mile or so away. Planes were still a fairly new invention then, exciting every time you'd see one.

It was also out there in the yard that Dad instilled in me a lifelong love of growing things and started my interest in horticulture, which would save my sanity one day far off, giving me something to do in prison camp. I remember Dad saying to me, 'If you're going to plant anything, plant a tree. A tree never gets tired; it grows day and night.' I guess he was a greenie before anyone knew what a greenie was. When I was nine or ten, I planted a row of pine saplings along our front fence. I'd find one growing somewhere, as they do all over Gippsland, and I'd dig it up with my hands and bring it home. The trees are still there, but many metres high now, more than seventy years old — nearly as old as me. I was a good gardener, too, even when I was young. I grew strawberries, onions and broad beans — I thought they looked lovely in their rows. I also kept fowls for the eggs. The chooks in their pens would mash up manure with their feet, and I would have to clean it out — barrow-loads of it — and put it on the strawberries. It was a hell of a job but we had strawberries for tea every night when they were in season.

It was Dad who instilled discipline in me, too. He was a precise man, and he taught me the importance of respecting the things you have. For instance, he was very particular about me washing and greasing the spade after I'd been working in the garden with it, so that it didn't go rusty. If I forgot, he would get out the razor strap and whack me around the legs! That frightened the hell out of me. But I learned my lessons, like the kids don't now. I didn't rebel.

When I was thirteen, it was clear to my parents that I wasn't much one for continuing on with school. In those days, unless you were going to give schooling a serious go, your parents simply couldn't afford for you to stay on. So I left and Dad found me a job on a farm, earning five shillings a week to look after cows and pick peas, helping a farmer who'd had to take a job at the butter factory to pay his bills. Times were tough, the middle of the Depression, and feed was scarce, so the cows were skinny things, their teats were sore and they were always cranky, often kicking over the buckets in the dairy. I found them difficult to handle, and I got pretty cranky myself — especially when they'd kick me. After about two weeks, my father visited while on his delivery rounds and asked how I was going. I said, 'Not too good.'

He said, 'You'd better come home.' He got me another job soon after, milking cows again, but for seven shillings sixpence a week, and board. But I wasn't there long before Dad found another, better opportunity for me.

'How would you like to be a butcher?' he asked. Dad had run a cutting cart before he married Mum, slaughtering and quartering on farms, so he knew a bit about the business. He said I'd be starting off delivering meat on horseback. I said I'd never ridden a horse with a saddle — only ever bareback or with an old corn sack to save ruining my trousers — but Dad said I'd get used to it.

I started in 1934, aged fourteen, on a day so rainy the Koo Wee Rup swamp flooded. I'd deliver meat in the morning, bread in the afternoon. The loads were heavy for a lad, and balancing them on the back of a pony was not a simple matter. Often, the horse would trip or rear and the meat would fall out of the basket and I'd pick it up, dust it off and put it back in the basket, and no-one was any the wiser. It became an education in itself. After a while, I could remember two days' worth of orders at a time, what they wanted, what they paid, and what they owed for meat and bread. It sharpened my memory — another skill that would serve me well in that time still far off. After two or three years of making these deliveries, I went to yard bullocks as well. I'd have to drive them through a bit of scrub to reach our paddocks, and I'd yell, swear, go crook at the dog, and crack

Young Ernie Brough, aged 12.

the stockwhip continuously. One day, Mr Welwood, who owned a nearby orchard, complained to my father about my swearing! But Dad understood. I would have to drive the bullocks into a yard, make sure I was quick to jump off the horse, and slam the gate after them — because they quickly sensed what the abattoirs were all about and didn't want to go in there.

I became a good horse rider. I had a horse called Chunder, a big roan, a magnificent stockhorse. You really had to hang onto him: he was like a quarter horse. I learned how to ride with my knees. The knees do all the work, the rest is balance. I reckon I could have ridden in a buck jump show and no horse would have tossed me off. Eventually, though,

I did all my deliveries on a bike. It was sad, but good economics — the bike didn't have to be fed.

Horses aside, I grew up with dogs — sheep and cattle dogs. I used to train them, then give them away; they were too good to be tied up in a backyard. I had one, a kelpie, who was a beauty. I'd go out to a farm somewhere, walk across a paddock, and halfway along I would tell him to sit. Then I would go on to the next gate, turn, and walk back past him to the gate we'd come in by, and still he wouldn't move. I loved it when dogs were as trusting as that. Of course, then I'd give him a whistle and in a split second he would be beside me, tail wagging furiously.

Mine was a typical country childhood and adolescence, but in the distance there was always a shadow: of the past lying over the future. We didn't need to look at Mum's photograph of her cousin Albert Jacka in his uniform to see it. Around almost every corner in Drouin were reminders of the Great War, which had ended in 1918, two years before I was born. The scoutmaster and funeral director in town were both survivors, and so were the Porter brothers, who owned and ran the general store. So was the manager of the Bank of Australasia, who had had half his jaw blown away in combat.

There was also a German in town, name of Bill Grohl. He had the saddlery. One day while I was on my delivery round, he said to me, 'You're not going to the war, are you?'

I said, 'I'm thinking about it, Bill.' It was 1939 and I was nineteen. He was much older, and I presume he'd been in the German army in World War I. He knew about war.

'Don't go — it's no bloody good,' he said. 'Don't go to war.'

2
SEE YOU LATER

For months in the middle of 1939, I'd been reading in the newspapers about how the Germans were giving the Poles a hard time, and about how bad the Nazis were, taking away the rights of Jews and such. I didn't know much about the world at large or politics then; didn't really know what was going on, but I kept thinking to myself, this is not right; this can't go on. The Germans already occupied Czechoslovakia. What were they going to do next? I was a kid who delivered meat and worked at the slaughter yards; I didn't know what it had to do with me, but I knew it wasn't right.

Life had changed a bit for my family by that time. My father had grown weary of humping around 200-pound bags of superphosphate and wheat. He was in his fifties then. I don't know how he ever did it. He and Mum packed up and moved to Myrtleford, in mountain country in Victoria's north-east, out of the Gippsland winds and about 200 miles away. Dad became an agent for Rawleigh's, who sold everything from coffee beans to mustards and spices to ointments and salves. I stayed on in Drouin, boarding and working, and, away from the good influence of my parents, I mucked up a bit more than I should have, occasionally having an ale or two more than was necessary, the way young blokes do.

I'd go hunting on weekends for deer, and foxes, too. When I was seventeen, I'd bought a long-barrelled .303, used in World War I, from a fellow called Pedersen, who owned a bike shop in Warragul. It cost me £3. I'd saved hard for it: I was only getting £3 9s a week then. I'd started going hunting regularly, mostly with my good mate Jack Walsh. We'd load up his old 1922 Citroën with the dogs — beagle hounds and a beautiful big Russian borzoi — and off we'd go, out to Wilsons Promontory on the coast to shoot hog deer in the swamps at Yanakie, or out to West Jindivick, at the headwaters of the Tarago, to hunt samba deer. I would learn a lot about guns and bullets and safety from the various blokes I'd go out with, and bush sense — we never had a compass, we knew where we were by the position of the sun and the terrain. And we were mostly lucky to have venison for dinner at the end of it. I'd butcher the meat myself, and sometimes take some back to the shop where I worked and pickle it — delicious.

Hunting party, doing our bit to keep
the local fox population down, 1939. I'm on the left.

One of our hunting companions was old Alec
McDonald, who lived out on the edge of the Labertouche
Ranges — wild, uncleared country. He used a US .44 under-
lever five-bullet magazine rifle that fired a lead bullet as big
as your thumb, and he had antlers hanging up everywhere in
the pine trees around his place. They weren't just souvenirs:
he lived off a lot of venison out there. Alec had been a sniper
in World War I, and sometimes he'd tell us about his time in
Palestine, scouting for the cavalry, going ahead into the wadis
there — the dry ravines formed by rainy-season streams.

Over lunch one day, he said, 'I'll never forget the first
bloke I shot. He was a Turk. He was coming round the bend

in the wadi and I shot him clean through the head. When we got to him, he had turned blue.'

Little did my mates and I know that within twelve months, we'd be over there, in the same wadis, guns in hand, too. At the time, all we were interested in was getting through the working week to get out hunting on the weekends, drink beer, and have ourselves a good time.

World War II broke out on September 3, 1939. We'd gone deer-hunting that day at Snake Valley, way out near Ballarat. We'd had no luck and were coming back through Melbourne that Sunday night in Jack's Citroën, with all the dogs in the back. The *Herald* banners were everywhere across the city: 'We Are At War With Germany.'

It wasn't a big surprise. For months, England and France had been warning Hitler to lay off Poland. Hitler said he would go into Poland if he felt like it. He signed a friendship pact with Russia, going halves in Poland, but Stalin was awake to Hitler: he moved all his troops into Poland, giving himself some breathing space. It was inevitable that England would go to Poland's aid when Hitler finally began his invasion on September 1. As our Prime Minister Menzies declared at the time, and as we all knew, it meant that Australia was also at war. Jack and I didn't talk about it that night except for an offhand comment or two: 'Suppose it won't be long till we're having a shot ourselves.' I don't know that either of us knew what to think.

A couple of my mates joined up immediately. I didn't. But I began to miss them and, as little by little others started joining up — the boy from the grocer's, kids I'd known from school, and especially a really good mate from school called Alan Lovejoy — I started to feel pressure to follow the mob. I had no idea of adventure or glory in my head, it wasn't about bravery or heroism or nationalism for me; it was more that niggling feeling that I should be doing something. Even though I was fairly naive at the time, I knew that what was going on in Europe just wasn't right. I wanted to do the right thing, I suppose. Somewhere in my mind was a bit of a dream,

The Drouin crowd, outside the Royal Hotel. Most of us in this picture joined up. I'm the one in the white shirt.

too, that I could do something to make my mum proud, be like her cousin Albert Jacka, bring home a medal, maybe even a Victoria Cross — not for me but for her.

I was in a bit of a quandary, though. To enlist, I'd have to ask my boss at the butcher's shop for a day's leave to go to Melbourne. That might not sound like a big deal, but in those days it was. There wasn't any such thing as a formal apprenticeship then for a young butcher, and you could be sacked for looking sideways if the boss felt like it. It wasn't uncommon to be sacked just for turning twenty-one, when the boss would have to start paying you adult wages. You had to prove you were worth keeping on. Now, if I took off to Melbourne for the day and was rejected by the army, that might be enough in itself for the boss to think twice about me — then I'd be left not only with the shame of rejection but without a job. And there was a chance that the army might reject me: after years of not brushing my teeth, my top choppers weren't too crash hot for one, and who knew why else they might not want me. Even though I had a good boss, Mr Winters, who liked me, I was pretty anxious about it, but I decided to try anyway, and one day, early in November, I asked for the day off. Mr Winters said all right, but he was oblivious as to why. Afterwards he asked his other assistant, who was about thirty-five, why 'young Ern' would be going down to Melbourne, and he replied, 'Don't you know, there's a war on?'

I hadn't told anyone what I was up to; not even Jack Walsh, who'd make his own decision to follow not long after me. I went by myself to Flinders Street Station, where there was a recruiting centre. The place was teeming and to say the least I was bewildered, just by the crowd. I was wearing a suit, of sorts, a walking fish out of water. When I got to the front of the line the officer asked me how old I was. 'Nineteen,' I replied. I hadn't realised that you couldn't sign up at nineteen, not even with your parents' permission. You had to be twenty. There were sixteen-year-olds who said they were twenty and signed their own papers, and the army was awake to them, sending them off back home, but I didn't know anything about it then.

The officer said to me, 'Well, couldn't you go for a walk around the block and be twenty when you come back?' So I did — and I was.

I wasn't called up straight away because of my rotten top teeth. I had to have them all pulled out and replaced by false ones. At nineteen! It wasn't pleasant: the dentist had to take a hammer to one of my back teeth to get it out, but that's what happens when you don't clean the ones you've got. I was fairly pleased with my new dentures, though. They looked a lot more handsome than the rotten ones and would serve me well for many years to come. Even better, Mr Winters, my boss, congratulated me on my decision by buying me a watch and telling me he'd keep a job for me there at the butcher's if he could for when I got home.

The Drouin Volunteer Fire Brigade. I'm the tall one in the centre at the back.

Finally, I was called up on March 28, 1940. I had my medical at a drill hall in Dandenong, and the doctor there said, 'I don't think you're right for the military — you've got flat feet.'

This annoyed me. I said, 'I'll tell you something. I go shooting deer — fifteen miles out in the bush every weekend. You come with me on a fifteen-mile hike, and we'll see who gets home first.'

And he said, 'Well, if that's your attitude, you'll be right.'

One thing I knew: I was physically fit. I played footy every weekend, for the Drouin seconds, often on cold, wet, muddy grounds in the Strzelecki Ranges, where it wasn't uncommon for a cow to wander onto the ground and we'd have to stop the game to shoo it away. I'd grown to be quite a big bloke — I'd been a short, tubby kid, but I was six foot one and lean now — and I played in the ruck. I was a terrible kick and a bit bandy-legged — I didn't get called Bandy Brough during school days for nothing — but I had a lot of fun. I was also in the Drouin fire brigade. We did competitions all through Gippsland and as far away as the suburbs of Melbourne. The fastest blokes would run with the hydrant to a 'fire' and get there before the cart turned up with the horses. I wasn't really an athlete like them. But I was fit and strong.

From Dandenong, my several hundred new mates and I went to the Melbourne Showgrounds, where we were given our uniform and boots. Most of it didn't fit: the trousers were too long, or too short, or too tight. You simply got what came next and had to swap with others until you had a kit in your size. I don't know what happened to that old suit I'd arrived in — probably went to charity. It was pretty overwhelming at first, suddenly being at close quarters with all these blokes I didn't know. Every sort of bloke was there: factory workers, bank clerks, labourers, tailors. It was all a bit weird, but at the same time, we were all in the same boat. We were all privates, and there was no leveller like being ordered to strip naked for another mass medical examination. We were lined up and this doctor made his inspection of each one of us, grabbing our balls and then poking around in our mouths and everywhere else — didn't wash his hands between victims. It sort of got our camaraderie off to a good start; you had to laugh.

We spent a couple of weeks training in Melbourne, at Caulfield Racecourse, then Williamstown Racecourse. We did long route marches, learned how to present arms, to use a rifle and to dismantle and rebuild a machine gun. I found this aspect of my new army life easy. I loved all the physical challenges, and even had a chance to show off on account of my good memory: in no time I could assemble a Lewis gun — an old-fashioned type of machine gun used during World War I — without thinking about it. It was nothing new to some blokes, those who'd already had training with the Citizen Military Forces — the equivalent of our Army Reserve today. There were quite a few, too, who'd gone through to high school and had had cadets training. Others just found this business boring — they'd rather have had a snooze in the sun than train. I suppose I was somewhere in the middle of the mob. I was taking this seriously — I knew these were things we had to do and learn — but with an eye open for a laugh. Some things did lend themselves to silliness. For drills, we used sticks rather than guns — there weren't enough guns to go around. For mortars — a muzzle-loading type of cannon that fires shells — we used an assemblage of blocks of wood and sticks. We called ours Wattlebark III, a very deadly weapon.

Mid-April, the middle of autumn, it was cold by the water on the bay at Williamstown, and the wind was whipping the damp over us. Everyone got the sniffles and there was snot on the ground everywhere. Camaraderie set in a little bit more solidly. At that stage there were about 150 men to my room, in what was the restaurant area of the racecourse, and we were all sneezing, coughing, hoicking and cursing. Being in such a crowd was still strange to me, but I was learning self-confidence among it, too. I had to. Coming from the country, I was unused to dealing with strangers, and was used to a level of honesty I wasn't sure I was going to get here. For instance, if you borrowed a few bob from someone in my home town, you paid it back, as a matter of principle. You wouldn't want to be known as someone who didn't honour a debt, and you wouldn't want to put a mate in the embarrassing position of having to ask for his money back, either. As it happened I'd lent one of my new army friends — a big redheaded bloke — five bob, which at the time was a whole day's pay, and he still hadn't paid me back when I heard he was about to ship out. He was a nice bloke but I wasn't sure if he'd just 'forget' his debt and go. So I fronted him and asked for the money he owed me. It took a bit of courage, but I did it. I got my five bob.

From Williamstown, we went to a camp at Balcombe on the Mornington Peninsula, as much to save us from pneumonia as to continue our training. There, we learned how to charge with a bayonet — effectively, to stick a bloke in the guts. We were using bags of straw but it felt odd. 'Charge,' the officer would call, and you would have to run to the bag and stick the bayonet in. If it jammed in the 'bone', you would have to fire the rifle to blow it off the bone. It didn't bother me too much: I was a butcher, after all. But I was troubled by the thought of having to do it to a human being. Plenty of others were troubled by that, too, and some couldn't do the drill at first. But we had to — line up, and charge again, endlessly. I realised that although this was all pretend, and I couldn't imagine for the life of me what the real thing would be like, these were drills that had to be learned so that they would be automatic when it came to battle. I didn't like it but it made sense.

At the end of April 1940, we went to Port Melbourne, all ready to ship out as the 2nd/7th Battalion of the 6th Division. But it was a false start. We were actually there to help load up the main contingent of the 6th Division, who'd come down from the camp at Puckapunyal. We didn't leave until September 15. By that time, we were all raring to go. In those five or six months of training and waiting to be off, I had become what you might call a sturdy soldier. I was as fit as it's possible for a young man to be, I was confident in myself, and somehow this new army life had simply become my life; this is what I was doing with it. On one leave in Drouin, I remember the bloke who owned the butter factory took a photo of me, and I stood tall for it, smiling and proud in my uniform. That's what it's like when you're nineteen or twenty, living in the moment, not thinking too far ahead. I wasn't excited by the prospect of battle, but I felt good about myself: I was doing the right thing.

Mum and Dad came down from Myrtleford to see me off. They were crying, but I was as callous as only a twenty-year-old can be. I just said, 'See you later,' then walked off. They hadn't tried to stop me from going. Their attitude was that if they didn't sign the permission form, I'd go anyway. I've always felt that I was a bit of a mongrel just to walk away like that. There was Mum, crying in the car, and I just walked off, '*See you later.*' But I didn't know then that it would be four years before I'd set foot on Australian soil again.

3
THE FIRE ON THE RIDGE

We set out from Port Melbourne the next morning on a Dutch freighter, and I thought I'd be one to get seasick for sure. I'd never travelled on a ship before, only ever been out fishing in nothing bigger than a ten-foot dinghy. That first morning we had pork chops for breakfast — the greasiest pork chops you'd ever eat — and I was waiting for them to do a job on me, all that pork fat sitting in my stomach, swaying with the ship … But it didn't happen. It happened to plenty of others though, particularly when we entered the waters of the Bight — the waves were twenty foot high. Incredible sight, but not for some. The blokes who had to sleep way down in the hull copped the seasickness worst. Fortunately, I was further up, on a deck where we slept in hammocks. I think that helped in getting accustomed to the movement.

The very worst of that journey remained the food. We had rabbit every day, and I mean every day, and while rabbit itself is a lovely meat if you butcher and cook it properly, this rabbit was nothing short of disgusting. Maybe they were trying to toughen us up, but to serve up rabbit with the entrails still in it was not in our best interests: it's unhygienic. Rabbit, with rabbit shit in it. Sometimes it's not an advantage to know exactly what it is you're eating. The highlight was the little slab of fruitcake we got each day; you'd hang out for it. There wasn't much else going on. We'd have rifle drills, six men at a time out on the deck. There wasn't enough space to really do anything, and it was a bit pointless; just something to keep us busy so we didn't go mad being trapped in this big tin can.

The whole trip took nearly four weeks. Along the way we pulled in at Fremantle, Western Australia, where we had a day's leave, and then we pulled in at Colombo, Ceylon, as Sri Lanka was then known, and had two or three days on shore. I remember being surprised there to see so many bullocks pulling wagons and so much cow manure all down the streets. It was a different world, a much poorer one, and we were warned to look out for thieves, though I didn't see any. Little kids would gather round us on the wharves and dive for coins we threw into the clear blue water for them. They were

At camp in Palestine, not long after arrival. The bandage on my knee
was the result of falling into a trench whilst chasing a soccer ball.

incredible divers and full of fun. Then it was back on the ship
and we didn't stop again until we got to the Suez Canal,
Egypt. The land we looked out at was desolate — desert sands
and flat — but I was amazed by the sheer size of the canal, a
hundred miles long, a great feat of engineering. We must have

been at the end of our boredom with ship life by then, though, because when we pulled in and a crowd of Egyptian kids gathered on the dock to wave and beg for coins, we did throw coins down to them, but heated them up with matches first so the kids would jump about and yell when they caught them. We were as juvenile as them, I suppose.

We disembarked at the Canal and from there we travelled in trucks through the Sinai Desert, on our way to Palestine. The trucks had been used for road-making and were still full of sand, dirt, dust and grit, and we were tossed about in them, twenty-five or so of us to a truck for about 150 miles or so, till we arrived at the headquarters of the 17th Brigade, where we would start training again. We didn't know what we'd be training for — the army never tells you things like that — but, boy, were we glad to be off that ship and looking forward to doing something.

Our camp here was about three or four miles from the coast, not far from the seaport of Ashkelon in what is now Israel, and there wasn't much but desert in between, only a few small mudbrick villages, which we were warned to steer clear of — not only for fear of thieves but because a local might stick a knife into you. In those days Palestine was under British mandate and it was a place in chaos — it still is today and for pretty much the same reasons: Arabs and Jews fighting each other. There was a British police outpost at Ashkelon, mounted police, who attempted to keep the peace, and often not very successfully. The

A British policeman patrolling the beach at Ashkelon, with the assistance
of a local recruit.

Jewish nationalist militia, called the Stern Gang, were fighting
both the Arabs and the British for sovereignty of the area, and
the Arabs were likewise intent on forcing the Jews and the
British out — and pinching British guns to do so. As a result, all
our rifles had to be locked up at night, and during the day you
had to keep your rifle with you at all times.

It was a situation that almost led to my imprisonment by
court martial not long after we arrived. I'd managed to get
dysentery, as many of us did, from the unsanitary conditions
of camp life. I was quite crook and light-headed because I had
the runs — food just goes straight through you — and I was
placed on light duties. Anyway, one day I'd just been to the

toilet for the hundredth time and I left my rifle standing against the latrine. Half-asleep, I completely forgot it was there and wandered off to get a drink of water. When I went back for it, of course the rifle had vanished. Well, for the next three or four days, did I get hell for it. I was looking at twenty-eight days in jail and I was questioned again and again by the captain in charge of my court martial as to what had become of my rifle. I had no idea. I was asked the number of my rifle and I gave it, or I thought I did. I must have been so out of it, I gave him the number all right, but backwards. As it turned out my rifle was eventually found, safe and sound, in the armoury: someone had picked it up and put it there. And, thankfully, once the issue of the muddled number was sorted, I got off, without charge. Needless to say, I never let my rifle out of my sight again.

The dysentery was taken care of with some medicine or other, white muck that tasted like diluted chalk, and it was back to training. Months of it we did there in the desert: gun drills, attack manoeuvres and long route marches with heavy backpacks on. We were kept busy every second of the day, from the moment we rose till we fell over at the end of it. On one occasion the commanding officer of our company, Captain Joshua, said to us: 'Come on, we're going to go out and have a look at some old geezer's tomb.' Great, another route march through the desert sand, we thought. But off we went, single file. It was always hard going, the sand would be

Striking a pose with some Arab kids on leave in Jerusalem. I'm on the far right.

up over your boots and the drag on your legs was painful, but that day the march seemed endless. We didn't see any tomb out there, just a few bits of stone strewn about. Some of the blokes were getting so buggered they couldn't carry their rifles. I was managing okay, just, and was carrying three or four of the rifles of those who weren't, when Captain Joshua must have realised he'd taken us out too far. Nothing else for it but to turn around and march all the way back again. At least a third of the group didn't: they slept in the desert that night. I made it back to camp, but by the time we got there our shirts were flecked with white from the salt that had leached out of our bodies. It was dreadful. The next day, Captain Joshua apologised. He said to us, 'I'll never do that to you again,' and he gave us all the day off. 'Do whatever you like,' he said. He was a good man, a bank officer in civilian life, and a wonderful military officer. Brave, too: he'd be awarded the Military Cross for his leadership at Tobruk.

It wasn't all work and no play there in Palestine. At times, we could get leave to go to the beach at Ashkelon, where it was relaxed and pleasant. Kids would come and cook us breakfast, and we'd go on a camel ride or two. It was all quite fun. Ashkelon was the site of an ancient city, too, and its remains could be seen in great black pillars of marble standing in the sand. Roman coins could still be found around there, too. I picked up a few of those coins on the beach, metal discs worn thin by possibly two thousand years or more of time. Back then I didn't think anything of it, though, and I'd toss the coins down onto the sand.

The surf at Ashkelon was more dangerous than it looked, with a strong rip. On one occasion some others and I were given the task of patrolling it — it wouldn't have done to start losing numbers by drowning before we got anywhere. I wasn't a strong swimmer — couldn't have saved myself in the event of being swept out — but it was our job to make sure no-one went out further than about knee-deep. We also had a week's leave in Cairo at one time, where I rode around the pyramids on a camel. Some blokes wanted to climb the great things; I only wanted to look at them so I could say, 'Yes, I've seen the Pyramids of Giza — and they're a big pile of rocks.'

That first Christmas away from home was a bit of fun too, though not exactly the type of fun the army approved of.

A Christmas postcard with a picture of my good self set in it, taken on leave in Jerusalem. Most of us had these cards made up to send home to family and friends.

A bunch of us on leave in Jerusalem again. I'm the second from the left, in front, and I've got a bottle of grog tucked into my shirt.

We'd had a decent dinner — some sort of forgettable roast — and then the canteen was open for beer. Well, all we had to drink it with was our dixies — the aluminium dishes we ate from — which were always greasy because there was never enough hot water to wash them in, and so an ideal breeding ground for stomach bugs. They were about as big as a billy, holding a litre or so. Some blokes got stuck into the ale — quite a few actually — and after three or four dixies full they were smashed. A predictable fight broke out, and it raged from about one in the afternoon till three — till some bloke pulled a bayonet on another and was arrested and sent off to detention. My platoon was on guard duty at the lockup and he asked two of our blokes if he could be let out of his cell to go to the toilet. They agreed and he escaped, later, rumour had it, to be picked up by the British military police in India. But those two poor blokes he'd made the slip from were court-martialled – twenty-eight days in prison for them. And quite a few long route marches ensued for the rest of us as a warning against irresponsible grogging and fighting.

My twenty-first birthday in February was a little more tame, but I did get a marvellous surprise. My mate from home, Jack Walsh, popped into camp to wish me a good one. Jack was with the 2/3rd Light Ack Ack and would soon be on his way to Greece. Geez, it was good to catch up with him, even if it was only for a brief while. It would be quite a long while before I saw him again.

Training and then some more, that's all we seemed to do, and still it would be a while before we'd be going anywhere

On manoeuvres in the desert near Marsa Matruh, having a rest from war games.

At camp in Palestine, waiting for our orders to be off.

to war. All these months of training and relentless discipline started to get frustrating, and impatience set in, to be going, to be let off the leash more than to get into battle. Other battalions and companies in our number had gone off to fight, but for some reason we were stuck there — either in Palestine or at another training camp at Marsa Matruh, not far from the Libyan border with Egypt. As I said, they never tell you why in the army. During this time I was singled out for corporal school and I wasn't told why about that, either. It wasn't until years later that I reckon I figured it out. It's the sound of your voice: it needs to be commanding. Only recently, I was lining up for a meal at the RSL club in Geelong when a bloke said to me, 'You've got a good voice. You should be on radio.'

Immediately, it put me back in Palestine. At the time, I was surprised, and a bit worried as to how I'd go. I didn't know if I had any leadership abilities in me.

There were fifteen of us chosen and the school lasted about three weeks. We had to learn how to throw our voices, yelling orders at each other across the desert dunes, and we had to know off by heart the procedures for instructing others on Bren gun assembly, rifle handling and control, and bayonet practice. My good memory served me well again for this sort of thing. I can still recite the booklet we got on the Bren gun, if you'd let me. Then we had to demonstrate our ability to give these instructions, in front of the officer in charge of us, Major Gwynne, and other bigwigs. We also had little tests of our strategic abilities, how well we could think on our feet. One day Major Gwynne said to me, 'Right, you've got a hill over there. There's a machine gun at each corner, and you're going to attack. How?'

I replied, 'I'd line up my machine guns so they're covering each corner … and then attack straight over the top of the hill.' It must have been a good answer. I ended up coming third in the class over all, and Major Gwynne wrote on the bottom of my certificate: 'Would make an excellent NCO.' For a bloke who'd never really ever seen himself as a soldier, let alone a non-commissioned officer, that felt pretty good.

But the main thing on my mind was: when are we going to get going? We were all tetchy. You can't keep blokes in that state of high expectation for months on end. You start to think, what's wrong with us? Aren't we good enough? We were jack of it. At one point, when my company was told we'd be shifted to a battalion that was part of the 7th Division, we got openly stroppy; we saw ourselves as part of the 6th. 'No way!' we complained. We were told to shut up and do as we were told or we'd all be split up and sent to the four corners of the earth. We shut up.

Six months we'd been waiting for our orders when they finally came at the beginning of May 1941. In the Mediterranean, Greece had just fallen to the Axis forces of Germany and Italy, while in Europe, France had fallen to Germany the previous June, and in northern Africa, for months the Allies had been fighting to recover territory in Egypt and Libya lost to the Italians earlier in the war. Over and over, the Allies had had to reconstitute and redeploy their forces to cover casualties and counter new challenges in the various theatres of war, and the flux of all that was the reason behind our long wait. Our battalion was originally supposed to go to Greece, but now we were told we would be going to North Africa. It meant that all our camouflage netting was the wrong colour, though — forest-green instead of desert-brown — and we had to change it by tying different-coloured ribbons onto the nets. We would be going now as part of the 2nd/32nd Battalion, which technically should have been part of the 7th Division, but was made part of the re-formed

9th Division because they were short a battalion. By that time we weren't complaining about which battalion or division we were in; it was a relief just to know we'd be getting into it at last.

Hitler had sent his Afrika Korps into North Africa, and the famous General Rommel had begun his counterattack against the Allies in March, seizing most of the long North African coastline. He attacked the strategically important harbour of Tobruk, but could not capture it, instead laying what became one of the longest and most famous sieges of the war, which would last from April until December.

We arrived at Tobruk in destroyers in the small hours of May 3, 1941. We had to move quickly: our boats had to be gone again by 2 a.m. or they would be vulnerable to German bombers. We had no aircraft of our own to cover us.

The Germans held all the high ground. Their guns were blazing, which made for a fiery and spectacular sight as we approached. There was a ring of fire on the ridge and it was mesmerising. No-one cried or carried on; tense anticipation gripped us all: what's going to happen here? We were all just looking up at that fire.

Now I was looking at it, anything I'd tried to imagine before was nothing like this; I couldn't believe it. That fire on the ridge …

I thought to myself: it's Gallipoli all over again.

4
NOTHING PERSONAL

Anticipation immediately gave way to adrenalin as they marched us up to a plateau above the harbour. And as the daylight gradually dawned, we lay there and watched as forty Stuka dive bombers came over, screaming like sirens. It was too overwhelming to be frightening; simply unbelievable. They circled then dropped three bombs each, sinking a South African gunboat in the harbour. But they couldn't destroy much in Tobruk itself because there wasn't much there. There was a hospital, but it was safely tucked away in tunnels built into a hill by the Italians. There had been a condenser on the beach, too, used to desalinate salt water, but the Germans had shot that up, so the navy had to continually bring in fresh water for us.

Stukas flying over Tobruk Harbour — the type of German bombers
that greeted us on our arrival.

That night, I went on my first patrol. This was it. No opportunity to say, 'Give us a chance to settle in!' You do as you're told, and I learned straight away that there's no other baptism in this business than a baptism of fire. I was with two other fellows, Jimmy Downes, a lieutenant, and Alec Harrison, a sergeant, who, like me, were both from country Victoria. Our mission was to move out about one and a half miles beyond our lines and stay there until daylight. The idea was that we would draw enemy fire so that the commissioned officer with the patrol, Jimmy in this case, could take compass bearings to learn more about enemy placements and the size of any force out there. Basically, we were decoys.

And I nearly shot Jimmy that night. I got disoriented, saw a movement in the darkness, raised my Tommy gun, and was going to blow the hell out of whatever it was. My blood was pumping that fast I couldn't hear myself think above the belting of my heart in my chest. I so nearly pulled the trigger. I'd learn fast that a lot of this sort of stuff happened, though no-one talks much about it, even now. Night-time, tense, trigger-happy soldiers, bullets flying all over the place in the dark. Accidents had to happen. Whose bullet kills whom? How would anyone have known? I never told Jimmy how close I had come to shooting him. In any case, he was killed a few months later at Tobruk.

But on that very first patrol, I learned my lesson to keep steady with the trigger. We completed our mission, stayed out until daybreak, all in one piece. We were walking back along a ridge towards our line when we saw three gazelles — beautiful gazelles in the midst of all this! What a sight they were! I made some crack about what a lovely meal they'd make but the beauty and the humour were short-lived, because as we kept walking, I happened to look behind us and saw a little black spot in the sky, like a blowfly, heading our way, at speed. It was a German fighter plane. That got the adrenalin going full bore again. Someone must have seen us and passed a message on to send a plane out to spot us. We were either going to be machine-gunned by the plane or intercepted.

There was no point in running; we were still too far from our line. And there was nowhere to hide. This was desert, with some tufts of grass, a ragged bush or two, but no cover. All we had for camouflage was the monkey suits we were wearing — khaki overalls — and the soft-soled, brown desert boots we were kitted with on patrol to reduce the sound of our footsteps. All we could do was lie face down and conceal our hands beneath us, and hope we blended in with the landscape. We lay longwise, in the direction the plane was travelling, because when a plane is travelling at high speed, anything lying longwise is harder to see. It worked. He flew straight over us, only about 200 feet up. But I don't think I drew breath again for the rest of that walk back, and when we

These sangers, or foxholes, are a way back from the front line, but they show how terribly shallow our 'trenches' were, and how exposed we were.

AWM 042473

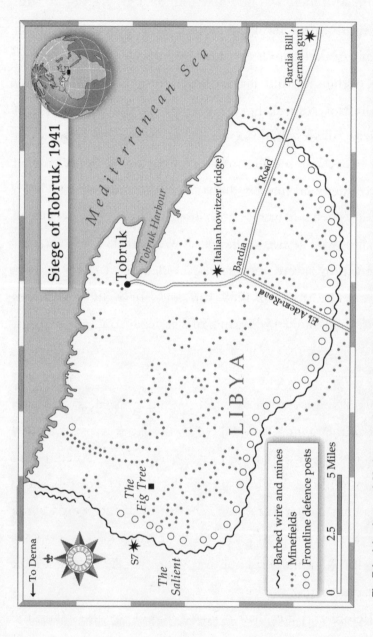

Siege of Tobruk, 1941

Mediterranean Sea

Tobruk

Tobruk Harbour

★ Italian howitzer (ridge)

Bardia

Bardia Road

El Adem Road

★ 'Bardia Bill', German gun

LIBYA

The Fig Tree

S7

The Salient

To Derna

Barbed wire and mines
Minefields
Frontline defence posts

0   2.5   5 Miles

The Tobruk battleground. My first patrol after we landed was about one and a half miles south from the lines at the El Adem Road. You can also see S7, just north of the Salient, where I was sent on that suicide mission when we lost Private Martin.

reached our line, back with our mob, I let out a sigh of relief and a half.

The front at Tobruk was only about ten miles inland from the coast and twenty across, and in the shape of a semicircle, surrounding Tobruk itself. Sometimes, the fighting was fearfully close, especially at the Salient, on the western side of the front, where there would be only thirty or forty yards between us and the Germans, nothing but a flimsy line of coiled wire marking our line. The Germans held the high ground there, too, and could survey us quite easily — they could see every move we made. It was the worst place to be. Wherever you were, though, the battleground was a terrible place because it was all rock. You could only dig nine inches into it, then build up a kind of barricade out of sandbags, rocks and bits of scrap iron for a foxhole, a one-man dugout, or a sanger as we called them. The arrangement meant that you were under fire all day. You would walk along a trench between the sangers thinking you were safe because it looked like you were in a trench, but it wasn't really a trench. It was only a slightly sunken passageway. Every night, I'd walk up to have a chat with a mate, and a shower of tracers would come down. You would never take off your tin hat — it was your umbrella — and a periscope was your eyes for having a look about out there.

Before this area had been won back by the Allies, the Italians had built concrete underground posts all over the place, but we weren't allowed to go into them. The thinking was that once you were underground and out of harm's way, you wouldn't want to come out again. You wouldn't fight. If you were on the surface, in a dugout, you had no choice but to fight. The underground posts were a bit of a trap anyway: the Germans cleared some of them using flame-throwers. My whole time at Tobruk I never saw anyone who refused to fight, though, or who crumbled under the pressure — not among us enlisted men, at least. No doubt some were terrified or horrified out of their minds at times, but they swallowed the fear. The thing is, among us, the fear seemed to run a poor second to the fact that we were in this together. I think, in an unspoken way, we held each other up. You couldn't give way, because you'd be letting your mates down. And if one of your mates was struck down, you stepped up to take his place; you didn't need an officer's orders to tell you to do so. We were nicknamed the Rats of Tobruk because we were trapped like rats in this ring of fire and because we lived in our shallow rat holes. But I think it might have been the way we kept at it, with our sense of brotherhood, that made the Germans call us rats with pointy teeth. We didn't have their tanks or their planes or some of their fancy weapons: we only had rifles, bullets, artillery and each other.

Not everyone on our side of the line was on the team, though. One particular senior officer comes to mind there. I won't name him, because I'm sure someone out there

We didn't have planes or tanks at Tobruk, only our guns and ourselves.
This picture shows our artillery blokes firing on German positions.

loved him. I didn't. One day, we'd been instructed to use a
jackhammer to try to dig a trench behind a small ridge. I'm
not sure why. It was either an exercise to keep us busy or to
suggest to the enemy that we were up to something at that
place. But it was driving us mad that day: the ground was
impossibly hard, and it became clear that we would have
to use commandeered Italian gelignite to break it up, a
dangerous exercise. This senior officer, a veteran of World
War I, ordered us to get on with the digging, reckoned we
weren't working hard enough at it. I was an acting sergeant by
then, a field promotion I'd been given when our sergeant, Jack
Reardon, was killed. Jack was a great bloke and maybe I had

a bit of fire in me over his death when I told that Senior Officer to get down there and dig the trench himself if he thought we were slacking off. I told him a bit more than that, too. I called him gutless and told him I'd never once seen him up at the Salient. He didn't say anything, but I reckon he had it in for me from then on; he'd find a special task for me later, to pay me back.

I had a bit of trouble with senior officers from time to time, with their attitude towards those 'beneath' them. Authority does strange things to some people. I couldn't help mouthing off occasionally, but mostly, I'd bite my tongue, as I did during another run-in with the unnameable Senior Officer. This time, some mates and I had gone down to the beach at Tobruk Harbour for a wash, and brought some sea water back in a big jerry can. The Italians had left behind some fibro-cement pipes, so we used them to build our own desalinator, boiling the water and then condensing it to clear it of salt. It was a marvellous piece of engineering if I do say so myself, and we got about two litres of beautiful fresh water from it. But Senior Officer came storming down, saying: 'Get that bloody thing out of the road. It looks like Dudley flats.' Dudley flats was a heavily industrialised part of Footscray, a suburb of Melbourne, where unemployed men lived in ramshackle humpies. I'm sure I looked daggers at him, but he had a point: the thing was quite a contraption and it was in the road. So we got rid of our home-made desalinator.

It was dealing with an enemy that you mostly can't see, though, that was constantly at the front and back of your mind. I remember one night, I'd dug a niche into the side of a ridge facing out over Tobruk, somewhere to have a bit of a sleep, and I had a terrible nightmare. I was wrestling with a German. He had a knife and was going to drive it into me. I was trying to get hold of him but I found that I was paralysed. I woke up with sweat dripping off me. And then, when I crawled out onto the ridge on my hands and knees, suddenly there was a German fighter plane coming straight over the hill. If I'd had a shotgun, I could have fired straight into the cockpit. The war was in my dreams and in front of my eyes; it was everywhere and everything.

That plane had been on a dawn run, probably to take photos of what we were doing, and whatever they had seen must have worried them, because the next day, they shelled us there. We were working away — digging that damn impossible trench again — when suddenly we heard four guns go off — an ear-splitting noise: Boom! We didn't know where it was coming from. The shells came straight over the top of us and exploded on the other side of the diggings, about thirty yards off, sending out a massive hail of shrapnel, which made us very grateful for the shelter of our trench, slim as it was. One in our party had gone for a crap at the time, and he came running towards us through the dust cloud, trousers round his ankles, screaming and swearing that he'd nearly copped it. Of course, we laughed our heads off. Humour inside this madness was as much a part of our armoury as anything else. But it was true: he was lucky to be alive; so were we all. The Germans hadn't been able to get the trajectory of the shells low enough to drop them right in on us. If they had, we'd probably all have been dead.

Somehow, I can't really explain how, you would get used to being under constant fire at the front. One night, I was shaking the dust out of my blanket and the next thing a shower of stuff came through and blew a hole in my haversack sitting next to me. The bullets went straight through the blanket but I didn't get hit. So much of it was sheer luck. Random, nothing personal about it. I think I realised early on that there was nothing personal in this business, nothing personal about a bullet, theirs or ours.

So much of the luck was freakish. One night, one of our soldiers, Bob Gannaway, left our dugout for a crap and was hit by a bullet that went through his helmet and stopped just a hair's breadth short of killing him. The force of the bullet dented and broke the metal of the helmet, jamming it into his skull and all he ended up with was a big lump on his head. He was fine. The helmet saved him, just. Another time during a German attack, a bullet hit another mate of mine, Dave Burge, in the helmet. Not only did it pierce the metal, but it slipped in between the metal and the leather fitting inside the helmet and spun around in there. Didn't touch him but the impact knocked him to the ground, and it had to hurt. He lay there for a moment, yelling, 'I'm going to die! I'm going to die!'

Dave was a tall, gangly bloke, arms and legs everywhere, he was, and Alec Harrison, our sergeant major at the time, and a shearer in civilian life, was unmoved. 'Get up, Burgy, and do a bit more fighting,' he yelled back. 'You're not dead yet.' And Dave did; he got up and did a lot more fighting.

I went on many more patrols at Tobruk to draw German fire. I learned to understand bullets. When they were making a whispering noise — *shoosh, shoosh, shoosh* — they were okay because they were further away. Of course, a stray one might still hit you, but they weren't directed at you. You knew they were getting closer when you could hear them make a cracking sound as they whizzed past your head, like a giant firecracker. Then you'd think each one was going to go through your head. One night early on in that first stint at the front, we attacked in bright moonlight and drew a storm of giant firecrackers. I think it was a bit of a stunt myself, to get everyone accustomed to a dose of it — no-one would have picked such a brightly lit night for a fight forty yards from the German front, but that was officers for you. The tracers came in so thick and fast that you couldn't see through them, and you thought every one of them was going to hit you between the eyes. Your eyes couldn't follow the line of the tracer, so you would see a streak of red, green or yellow coming at you — and then suddenly, it would go off in your ear hole: 'Crack!'

Stretcher-bearers at Tobruk. I'll never forget the courage of those blokes.

AWM 020743

For some reason I didn't ever worry about getting shot. I was never afraid of the bullets. I got used to them; it was all in a day's work. I thought I was lucky, and I was. But when I think back on it now, I should have been petrified. It would only ever have taken one errant bullet, one ricochet, and that would have been the end of me. It was for so many others. I wasn't frightened of the artillery, either: it had to land right on top of you to do any damage. Aerial bombing was the same. The most important thing during a bombardment was to flatten yourself on the ground so as to avoid the shrapnel. Maybe there was just a sort of subconscious logic helping me out: if I wasn't afraid, then my luck would hold; if I was killed, well, I wouldn't be around to know about it. But I don't know. It wasn't bravery; it was more a way to justify to myself what was happening, I think.

I saw many, many brave men, and not all of them were combat soldiers. One night, a runner had directed me back to my dugout, and just as I got there, a bloke from another battalion was shot through the back of the knee and collapsed in front of me. I was about to pick him up and put him in the dugout when two stretcher-bearers came along and yelled at me: 'Get in the bloody hole, or you'll be next!' I did as I was told. And they were unbelievably brave, those stretcher-bearers. They were in the thick of it like us, but didn't carry rifles. In daylight, they'd carry a Red Cross flag while they were picking up the dead and wounded, which meant the

Germans would not shoot at them. But at night — when most of the battles were fought — it was impossible to tell them apart from other soldiers, and they were as much targets as we were. Nonetheless, not many stretcher-bearers got the Victoria Cross.

Most brave men don't get VCs, and most of the business of war has little to do with bravery.

~

We'd spend three weeks at a time at the front line. Conditions were frightful. As I've said, the ground was rock-hard, the dugouts were shallow, sandbags and rocks not offering too much in the way of further protection. And it was stinking hot most of the time. The dugouts were full of flies and fleas. The only way to get rid of the fleas was to pour out half a cup of petrol into the dugout and put a match to it to burn them out. It would work for a few days, but they always came back.

There were no toilets. When you had to go, you took a walk and a shovel, and buried your business. At least that helped to keep the flies down. It also cut down the spread of diseases. Nonetheless, in quick time everyone had dysentery and malnutrition sores, because there was no fresh food. These sores, often about as big as a thumbnail, were so tender you could hardly bear to touch them. They'd form on the joints

This is what the battleground looked like after an offensive action — a garbage tip.
We'd salvage what we could, of both men and equipment.

Some of our blokes from the 9th Division at Tobruk, looking, and no doubt feeling,
a bit the worse for wear.

— knees, elbows and wrists — and before going out on patrol you'd think, how am I going to crawl out tonight with these screaming sores on my knees and the runs? But the adrenalin would kick in and you wouldn't think about them again till you got back, when the pain from the sores would return, along with the runs. We were all on ascorbic acid tablets, vitamin C, which we'd be given every few days or so to avoid scurvy, but really, we were in such a pitiful state, the lot of us, I reckon if the Germans had known and staged one big, concentrated attack, they'd have flattened us.

You couldn't shower, shave or change your clothes for three weeks at a time, either. I had no shirt; my only one fell apart in the dirt. I had a sweater, a pair of service trousers cut off at the knees with a knife, and an overcoat. I had no underclothes, and no socks in my boots. Like most of the guys, I wore one sock under my helmet, pulled over my head like a beanie, to keep the cold out at night: this was desert, remember — stifling during the day, freezing at night — and we'd all had our hair razored off so that we didn't have to wash it. Couldn't wash anything. The time the bloke had been shot through the back of the knee in front of me, his blood was smeared across my legs and trousers, and it stayed there for weeks. That was how it was all the time in the sangers.

We must have smelled bloody awful — just our breath alone must have been noxious — but we all smelled the same so it didn't matter. You had no choice but to get used to not washing. If you were lucky, you might get down to the beach on a spell away from the front. You would take your shirt (if you had one) and wash everything at once. There were no towels, no ablution benches, nothing. Dirt and sand became a part of your being, as it had been since we arrived in Palestine. I remember before we left for Tobruk and we were waiting for our orders at Marsa Matruh in Egypt, the desert dust, fine as talcum powder, would blow in under the tent all night long; and at Tobruk the dust storms were mammoth, sometimes lasting as long as three days. Dirt and sand were so ingrained on us that you didn't notice it, really.

Every morning, we were woken an hour before dawn — if, that is, we'd managed to be asleep — and we'd be ordered to stand to, with rifles at the ready. This was always a trial — the coldest hour of the freezing desert night was the one before dawn, just as we were being rudely awoken. But it was a necessary precaution. War is a day-and-night around-the-clock business, and the likeliest time for a surprise attack was just before sunrise. It was in our interests to be ready.

We were always hungry. All we had to put in our stomachs was a bottle of water a day and a stew that was made by cooks on the waterfront at Tobruk Harbour and brought up by runners at night. It was a concoction of such delicacies as tinned bully beef and mutton and veg, but I didn't know what its secret ingredient was until one night I was down on the beach and observed the cooking in action. I had never seen so many flies in my life, and they'd get caught in the steam floating up from the pots and meet their demise in our dinner. I realised then what we'd been eating for three weeks: fly stew! My mother sent me a cake every month, but not one of them reached me. I realised later that they had probably all gone to another soldier called Brough, not a relative and not on the same front. He mustn't have asked any questions. In his shoes, I probably wouldn't have asked any either!

Water was always in short supply. Our one bottle a day was around one litre. The water cart would come up from the beach at night and we would fill up our bottles. But often the navy could not get enough fresh water in on their run, so they would top it up with salt water. Sometimes it was so salty that you couldn't drink it. But somehow, you had to: there was no other water.

Alcohol was virtually nonexistent. One afternoon, we were given one warm bottle of beer between every three soldiers, the only ration of alcohol we ever got at Tobruk. A soldier in my group was Noel Stephens, from Warrnambool, a God-fearing man and a teetotaller. He was contemplating his mug of beer when another man, knowing Noel's abstemious nature, came up and offered him £10 for his beer. It was a notional £10, of course, to be paid later; none of us were carrying money. Noel thought about it for a moment, then shook his head and slowly drained his mug. These were desperate times; this was a desperate man. The odd thing was that being at war actually helped some men. Alcoholism was a disease not much discussed or treated back then. Some men joined the army with the blue faces of hardened alcoholics, and months later had more regular complexions. In all ways, they had found the desert dry. It cannot have been easy for them. But nothing about our situation was easy.

As for entertainment, you had to make your own. There was plenty of toilet humour, obviously. I remember one day this bloke was doing a crap, so relaxed about it he was, he was even reading a bit of newspaper. Another bloke snuck up behind him with a shovel and pinched his poo, so that when this relaxed crapper stood up to bury his business, he found nothing there. He went off his head with confusion, and we all found that hilarious. There was plenty of black humour too: one of our cooks, name of Jack Lucas, after being told to clear up his area of empty tins — mainly tins of Libby corned beef that he was adding to the fly stew — buried them in a heap the shape of a funeral mound and stuck a cross on it, with RIP written in the centre and a makeshift plaque below that read: 'Here lies Libby, 10,000 miles from home.'

There were more dangerous types of fun, as well. Some of the artillerymen would 'play' with an abandoned Italian howitzer under the lip of a ridge on the El Adem road, in the southern part of the battlefield, where the lines were much farther apart. They would stoke it up with whatever they could find: charges, surplus ammunition, any old explosive, and this howitzer had a barrel on it big as a shark's mouth. Then they would detonate it, to see how far they could make it go. It made for a pretty spectacular fireworks display some nights. It was not the sort of game you would be advised to play in your own backyard and it probably sounds puerile, but boys were just being boys. It was not as if we could pop down the road to the pictures or up the road to the pub. This was a war zone and we were never far from the action. You couldn't help but be aware of your mortality. You had to have ways to let off steam. Besides, it must have made the Germans wonder sometimes what the heck was going on.

But one night the boys went too far. They stuffed everything they could find into the howitzer and it blew up. Fortunately, no-one was hurt — except one poor bloke walking past who copped a whack on the bum with a piece of flying metal which gave him a nasty bruise. Needless to say, that was the end of that game.

Not so the war games. They ground on and on, but pretty soon I was about to take an unfortunate leave from them.

5
BACKSIDE ON THE LINE

A good soldier should never get shot in the head; he should always have it down. And I always did keep mine down — head tilted towards the ground, eyes peering up under the rim of the helmet. The rest of your body remains vulnerable, of course, some parts more so than others. Now, I was quite a big fellow then, not just tall, but solid, especially around the rump — such an ample rump I had that on the ship on the way over from Melbourne, the running joke in my battalion was that I would never get shot in the head, but I might cop one in the backside. I laughed, too. I figured that I could live with a couple of holes in my arse but not in my head. Little did I know …

I had been in Tobruk for nearly three months when I was

Getty Images 50621331

The township of Tobruk, looking the worse for wear. What a waste.

sent out on what was basically a suicide patrol. Two other fellows and I were to go out into the heavily fortified Salient, held by the Germans, find a fork in the road, camouflage ourselves and count the trucks that went by. We had no map, no compass, no water bottle, no camouflage groundsheet, just ourselves and a rifle each. Oh, and a grenade. I had one grenade, and that was a novelty. It was the only grenade I would carry at Tobruk.

The officer who sent us out was the unnameable Senior Officer, whom I had clashed with previously when trying to dig that impossible trench out of the rock. I'm convinced to this day that he carried a grudge against me and saw this as his chance to act on it. That sort of thing wasn't unknown in the army. A very good mate of mine in Geelong, a fellow veteran and the type of bloke too modest to want his name in a book, once said to me he thought a good number of officers in war were shot by their own disgruntled troops. It would only take one bullet, he said, and no-one would ever know where it came from. I'm sure he's right. I know of at least one account where a senior officer was threatened by a junior officer for working one of his soldiers too hard, sending him out on dangerous missions nine nights in a row; a form of abuse, really. 'Send him out again and I'll shoot you,' the junior officer said. Anyway, the reality this night for me was that I would soon be dead or a prisoner of war; either way, my favourite Senior Officer would be rid of me.

I said to the rest of the boys as the three of us went out: 'That's it. You won't see me again.'

I could smell the bullets coming over even before I left the dugout. Normally, we faced tracer bullets, which hissed through the air and down into the sangers and dazzled you. But it was machine-gun bullets that opened up on us this night, a hail of them from four guns, pellets whizzing everywhere, deafening, in the light of red flares going up and the flashes of the guns and mortars. The two fellows with me were privates: Hargraves, who'd been in Tobruk for as long as I had, and Martin, who'd only been with us for a couple of days. This was Private Martin's first patrol, and it killed him just about instantly, I think. He was from Longwarry, near my home. I caught a glimpse of him, on his knees, his rifle up on his shoulder, like he was in training on manoeuvres, he was that inexperienced, frozen probably, as uncertain as I was on my first patrol, and there was nothing I could do about it. I couldn't look behind me again to check, I thought he was still with us, but he wasn't. I could see Hargraves about ten feet away, and, like me, flat to the ground, but not Martin. I thought, he's gone. It wasn't fair at all for him to have to face that as his baptism, as if there is anything fair about any of it; I'll always regret not getting in touch with his people at home to tell them about it when they wrote to me asking, but a lot of things like that happen after war is over; it's too hard to talk about them.

I suppose Hargraves and I had been over the wire only for about five minutes, and in that time, he was shot through the foot and I got one in the left arm. That got me, I thought when the bullet hit, but it only felt like a short, sharp burn.

That's how mad the effect of adrenalin is. The next bullet that got me, however, in the next fifteen- or twenty-second burst from the machine guns, cut through my body's pain defences like nothing else. Where did it hit? Straight through the right cheek of my arse, of course, the highest point of me at that moment. It was as if someone had laid into me with a log, a sledgehammer blow.

I didn't know how badly I was wounded, but I knew I had to do something, keep on with the job. My instinctive reaction was to raise my Tommy gun and pour about fifty rounds into that German machine-gun post. I threw my grenade in on top of them as well. I could feel the ground shake as the grenade exploded, we were that close. It was a desperate act for a desperate moment.

They must have run out of ammunition, though, firing four machine guns at once, and there was no response. They wouldn't have known I'd had just that one grenade, either; they, like us, wouldn't have known what was coming next. So I grabbed Hargraves, and we started to head back towards our lines, or at least in that general direction. His foot and my arse were no impediment to getting out of there. We followed the North Star because I knew that was the direction of the Mediterranean and our lines, and after about twenty minutes, heart going like the clappers, not really knowing that we were anywhere except within the siege area — which was booby-trapped all over with mines, theirs and ours — we heard the sound of digging. I said to Hargraves, 'If they're Germans, we'll take them on.' What else could we do? I had about twenty rounds left — nothing. But we'd not go without putting what we had into them. They weren't Germans, though; they were our own men. Somehow we'd got there, back to our lines, that night. I heard the sound of Captain Joshua's voice and realised we'd not just found our lines, but company headquarters. Geez, I thought, someone's been looking after us.

One of the first blokes I saw when I got back into our nest of rat holes was Bert Cocks, another country boy, from Nathalia, Victoria. I'd been at corporal school with him and I'd be best man at his wedding one day, but at this moment, when he saw me he just laughed at the blood round and down the back end of me: 'Got you at last?' He was one of those who had always reckoned I would end up getting shot in the backside and here I was. I didn't get much sympathy. I didn't want sympathy. Getting wounded was all part of the business. If you didn't think of injuries that way, you would never put your hand up in the first place, let alone your backside on the line. Besides, worse had happened that night: Martin never came back.

It was July 30, 1941, a date I've never forgotten. Thirty years later, another mate and Gippsland boy whom I'd met back in Balcombe training camp, Arthur Byrns, would run into me at Geelong RSL and ask, 'Excuse me, but did you ever get shot in the arse?' I'd reply, 'Yes,' and he'd say, 'Well, in that case, I know you. You were my old sergeant.' And boy, yes, I had been shot in the arse.

It was a good thing Hargraves and I had ended up at headquarters because there were ambulance officers right there. They put me on a stretcher and it was straight into a vehicle to the hospital for me. At that time, the great surgeon-soldier Weary Dunlop was working in the tunnels of Tobruk hospital. I don't know whether or not he dealt with me, because when I got there and it was clear the medicos couldn't patch me up on the spot, they knocked me out to have a better look at the wound. I remember the smell of the chloroform and being told to count to ten: I got to seven before lights out. Somehow, while I was there, my watch, the one Mr Winters, my boss at home, had given me, went for a walk. I never saw it again. I was pretty cranky about that.

As expected, the wound on my left arm wasn't too bad, but the one in the rump was quite a bit nastier. No broken bones, fortunately, but on the way through, the bullet had torn the muscle and split my skin open — not a neat wound. I'd have to be sent off to the Australian General Hospital on the Suez Canal for a further look. At the time I was more amazed to find, when I woke up from the anaesthetic, that I'd been stripped and given a wash while I was out to it, and my skin had turned white. I didn't realise just how dirty I'd become from the desert dust. I'd turned berry-brown out there and thought it was a suntan.

My evacuation from Tobruk was a bit of an adventure in itself. The Germans had a big naval gun called Bardia Bill, which they used to shell our destroyers in the harbour and disrupt our supply lines. It had a range of ten miles. While the hospital was located in the lee of the land, and was safe, the harbour wasn't. Our blokes would use barges and small craft to load and unload the ships, and I was lying on a stretcher

AWM 010992

These small boats would run the gauntlet of the German guns and bombing raids to punt men and supplies to and from our Allied ships. We wouldn't have survived, much less fought, without the support of those navy blokes.

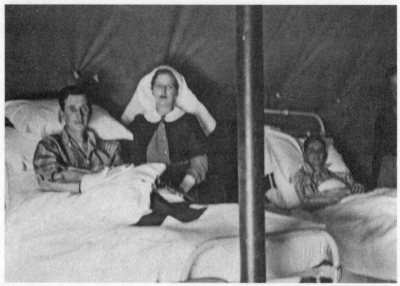

A ward inside one of the tents of the Australian General Hospital at Suez Canal.
The chap looking at the camera doesn't look too happy to be there — I'm sure
I didn't either, during my stay.

AWM P00224.001

on one of those barges when a shell came over. It made a screaming noise and there was shrapnel everywhere. All I could think was that you were meant to stay low and I couldn't get any lower than this. I suppose some of our guys were hit. As I've said before, it was a lottery, random, all about luck. There I was, injured but safe, while others were dying.

After about three days at the General Hospital in Egypt it was decided I'd have to have a couple of stitches put in, as the wound wasn't healing as quickly as hoped; it wasn't closing up properly on its own, and that sort of thing risked an infection getting in there. The doctor said to me, 'It'll only be quick. Reckon you can take it without an anaesthetic?'

I said, 'Sure. Go on. I can take it. Just get it over with.' I was offered a whisky beforehand and for the life of me I don't know why I knocked it back. When the doctor got going with his needle I certainly could have done with it. He was quick, but it damn well hurt!

The following day I was moved out to a rest camp near Tel Aviv on the Palestine coast and was there for a couple of weeks before I got my next orders. I was to report for duty further down the coast at a training base camp south of Gaza. I did as I was told, but I didn't want to return to duty. It was my moment of cowardice. I didn't want to go back to war. I turned up at this base camp, though, but I didn't report straight away. When I got there, I wandered into the baggage tent and stayed there all day. I don't think I knew what I was doing. Hedging, I suppose. I had no intention of deserting, I was just stuck for a bit. I stayed there till the next day when someone came in, asked what I was doing there, and said I'd better come out for parade. I did. And I reported for duty. If you were to look at my military record you'd see I was 'missing' for two days. I didn't get into trouble for it. I hadn't refused an order; I just hadn't turned up on time.

I was a fully fledged sergeant by now, and was given eighty reinforcements to take back to Tobruk. After I got these orders, that was it, that was what I was doing: getting on a train with eighty blokes, 200 miles back across Egypt. The responsibility kicks in. I'd learned a bit by that time about handling men and giving orders. Some love you, some hate you and tell you to get stuffed. You can't take that personally. On the battlefield, there's not much time for arguing a point, but eighty fresh reinforcements are another matter. On this train trip back through Egypt I'd learn that some men just don't listen to good sense.

Before we left Palestine, I'd warned this mob about falling prey to local rip-off merchants. While Australians, unlike the British, were regarded as no-one's enemy — in fact, we were well known for getting along with all sides in the mess that was Palestine — we were as fair game as anyone for a trickster. And, likewise, on the train through Egypt I told the boys not to buy whisky from the local kids who'd be peddling grog around the stations we stopped at, because what they'd really be buying would be either a bottle of donkey's urine or cold tea. Well, one fellow among us, a fellow from Kalgoorlie called Tom, thought he knew the lot. 'I know all about whisky,' he said. 'I'll be right.' The next day, when we pulled in at a station, I saw him running around the platform like a blue-arsed fly, brandishing a bottle of Dewar's scotch. I asked him what was going on. 'I'm chasing that bloody little Arab,' he said. 'He sold me a bottle of cold tea!' It had cost him ten shillings, silly bloke, and the kid, predictably, had disappeared into the crowd.

We got back on the train and continued our journey across the Nile Delta — an amazing place. I stared out the window at the maize crops growing there, for forty or fifty miles, as far as the eye could see. It was beautiful, seeing all that grain growing in the middle of all that desert. Something to take your mind off what we were going back to: the front.

6
WHEN YOU MIGHT BE DEAD TOMORROW

We sailed from Alexandria back to Tobruk on a destroyer in the first week of September. The siege was still on, and while the eighty men I brought over were divvied up as reinforcements to this platoon and that, I rejoined my unit. Straight away I saw nerves and tempers were becoming frayed — the state of them, all sick and tired, literally, and I knew in no time I'd look and feel like that again too. Our lieutenant, Jimmy Downes, had been killed by a bomb on the beach, and our sergeant had been killed at his post in August. That left me in charge of our platoon, which, at strength, was thirty men.

We were at a place called the Fig Tree, a relatively safe area about a half a mile back from the front line at the Salient, when a new officer came down to us. He was a young bloke, a lieutenant, probably straight from Duntroon Military College by the look of him, and he was pompous and arrogant from the first. Again, I won't name him, but he was another one, like the other, elder Senior Officer, who was big on giving orders but shy of going to the Salient himself.

'Sergeant,' he pulled me up one day.

'Yes, sir?' I replied.

'You're going to make up the water rations at this post,' he said.

Now, at this particular post there had been a reserve of water kept in two-gallon cans, in case we became cut off from the main supply, and those from the battalion who'd been here before us had drunk it. My back was up immediately, because what the officer was suggesting was that we refill the water at the post from the one measly bottle of water we each got a day. 'Why?' I said to him. 'We didn't drink it.' And he wanted to argue the point with me. Well, I became worked up quite quickly — he wasn't going to take a drop of water from my blokes. I told him, as I had my previous favourite officer, that he was gutless, never seen him up at the Salient, unlike real officers, such as Captain Joshua. And I might have added a few other choice words as well.

He fumed. 'I'll have you court-martialled,' he bellowed.

'Righto, you do that,' I replied.

He stomped off and came back a little while later with the sergeant major — our Alec Harrison, the shearer. 'What's the trouble?' Harrison asked me. As sergeant major, it was part of his job to mediate in disputes such as this, between officers and their men. I told Harrison the story. I said I wasn't going to stand for penalising our blokes when they had done nothing wrong. I told him I was doing the right thing by my men. After a while, Harrison said to the officer: 'Okay, come on, come with me.' And I never saw Young Officer Duntroon again.

That situation with the water was just plain silly, uncalled for, but it's the state of war itself that puts people in impossible situations, all the time asking things of you that you don't want to do. While I'd been out of Tobruk, at that rest camp near Tel Aviv, my friend Arthur Byrns had come up against his own impossible situation. He was a Bren gunner in my platoon, and during an attack on an Italian post, he came across an enemy soldier who refused to come out of his dugout. Arthur's commanding officer at the time yelled at Arthur to get him out, and Arthur tried, but still the Italian wouldn't budge. So the officer said: 'Shoot the bastard.' Fortunately, just at that moment, a projectile — a ricocheting bullet perhaps, or a piece of shrapnel — hit Arthur in the left arm, bowling him over. It hurt like hell, but at least it meant he did not have to shoot the Italian as per orders.

AWM 020271

One of the many ships that steadfastly serviced us troops at Tobruk.

We stayed in Tobruk only three more weeks. The whole of the 9th Division was pulled out, too depleted to go on. Every man was underweight, ill and battle fatigued. We were relieved by Polish and Czech battalions, who were keen as mustard to have a go at the Germans, and British battalions would join them as well — but it would be another three months yet before the siege was over and Rommel was driven back.

We of the 9th Division were bound for Palestine once more, and I'll never forget what great blokes the navy fellows were who brought us out of Tobruk on their destroyers — the *Vendetta*, the *Waterhen*, the *Voyager* — just a few of the ships' names I can remember. They were ready with cups of

This is me at corporal school in Palestine. It's a pity the photo is a little too blurry for you to see how chuffed I was to have been recommended for promotion to NCO.

tea and sandwiches as soon as they saw the state of us. We would not have survived without them at Tobruk, there would have *been* no Tobruk without them: they were the lifeline of the army, and doing their job like clockwork — dodging the German shelling and keeping us supplied with everything.

Once in Palestine we were all given plenty of leave. But I was sent off to an NCO cadre for a few weeks to learn whatever else I needed to know as a non-commissioned officer. We learned map reading and control of troops; they were watching how good your sense of command was. There was always someone looking at your credentials in the army, sizing you up, testing you to see what to do with you next — not that you'd ever be told this was going on, of course. At this NCO school, along with the usual route marches and exercises, they also had us playing a lot of soccer and rugby. After our experiences at Tobruk, it all seemed a bit pointless to me, and to be honest I didn't take much notice of the drills or the games, just did as I was told. And the classes on leadership seemed too academic after what I'd just come out of; I quickly got sick of it. School never was my thing. I took every opportunity to get down to the canteen to get some grog into me. Remember, I was only twenty-one.

I spent that Christmas of 1941 in Palestine, and at that time the war was changing again, dramatically. The Japanese had bombed Pearl Harbor earlier that month, and there was a feeling among us of: how the hell are we going to win this thing now? Many Australian troops were sent home after Pearl Harbor, to fight against the Japanese, who were advancing rapidly through the Pacific. This lowered the mood further for those of us left behind. Others were going home to defend *our* territory, *our* part of the world, and we of the 9th Division were left here in the desert. Little did we know what our compatriots would soon face at the hands of the Japanese.

Those of us in the 9th Division were sent instead to Lebanon, to a place called Ramleigh, near the port of Tripoli, not to be confused with the city of the same name in Libya.

Army command decided to send us on manoeuvres with the 7th Division in the mountainous country in the north of Lebanon, for large-scale mock battles — as usual we didn't know why. A battalion of Nepalese Gurkhas of the British army was waiting for us with mules to pack. We learned new tricks from them: for instance, simple things like pulling the sleeves of your overcoat inside out meant you could roll your coat tighter to make extra room in your pack; and more essential things like making sure the water cans we carried were filled to the very top so they wouldn't slosh and rattle and cause the mules to stampede. We set off through the olive groves in the countryside and found we still had plenty to learn. The mules would stampede, our machine guns kept falling off, and the Gurkhas would have to go back to retrieve them. While we were out there, one battalion from the 7th Division became a ghost force: it got lost and we never saw it again. It turned up later half a world away on the Kokoda Track and did a very good job.

Next, they had us digging fortifications on the main road north from Lebanon to Syria. This was in preparation for an expected push by the Axis forces from the east. Germany and its allies were intent on taking Stalingrad and had advanced into the Crimea. The Germans also had a friendly arrangement with 'neutral' Turkey, which seemed certain to give up its neutrality if Hitler succeeded in Russia — the Turks were poised on the Black Sea, waiting. It seemed a

Me and a mate having a wash at Tripoli, Lebanon.
There's no modesty in war! But the wound in my rear had healed up nicely.

Digging those fortifications in the north of Lebanon. Hot and thirsty work, to say the least.

house of cards waiting to fall, and if it did so it would fall like a ton of bricks on the Middle East, on us.

So we were labouring away in the Syrian desert, the hottest place I've known. It could get up to 120 degrees Fahrenheit some days — that's 50 degrees Celsius. We'd go out in trucks and dig these fortifications — a great big hole in the side of a hill for a headquarters and dugouts. Even Arabs don't do such work in the heat of the day, and one day I crawled under one of those trucks to try to escape it. We spent three or four weeks at it.

Then we spent about three weeks doing training devised by a British army unit called the Long Range Desert Group

— desert navigation and reconnaissance. I think it was designed to see how little water a man could function on before dying of thirst. In the evenings we would rendezvous and a water tank would come in. The officer in charge would have his revolver out while we went to fill up our bottles, as a menace to those who might go back for seconds. It was a bit of an act, a pretence at British discipline, and unnecessary. But we all played along with the rules of the water game, the basic idea of which was for each soldier to work out for himself how to survive on minimal water in such searing heat. I used to walk a couple of metres away and drink the whole bloody lot. I figured that at night I wouldn't sweat as much as during the day, so I would get more benefit from the water

One of our trucks in Syria, during our Long Range Desert Group training.

then. If I saved it for the next day, I would sweat it out almost as fast as I drank it. Mind you, I would do it hard at the end of the next day when I saw blokes draining the last of their water bottles knowing mine was empty.

There were times, though, when discipline was an issue. We were not on the front line of war, but we were in war mode and mood. There was much belligerence, and the heat didn't help. One day, when we were sent to guard a storehouse of iron pickets, barbed wire and other supplies for the engineers, one of our ranks, a bloke called Percy, got drunk. He must have got his hands on some of the beer the Arab kids would peddle to us, and he began shouting and carrying on about the officer in charge, Lieutenant Matt O'Meara, saying

Ping-pong in Lebanon —
a moment of friendly sport amid fraying tempers in the desert.

what a rotten dog he was and what have you. I don't think Percy realised that O'Meara was in hearing range, when suddenly O'Meara appeared from a tent, telling Percy to shut up and pull his head in. Percy didn't. 'C'mon, I'll clean you up,' he screamed and so O'Meara stripped off his shirt as if to say this was not officer versus private, but man to man. Then he proceeded to give Percy the mother and father of a hiding. We stood around and cheered like schoolboys. Percy, chastened, did not say another word. O'Meara, sad to relate, was later killed at El Alamein.

War, with all its death, and its tension between violence and discipline, does strange things to a man's psyche; even off the battlefield, it becomes too easy to lose sight of the value of life. One day, back in Lebanon, I'd been hitchhiking to the beach for a swim and was picked up by some other Australians in an army ute. A little further down the road, our way was blocked by a flock of sheep. Rather than slow down and wait, the driver tore down one side of the flock, tooting all the way, hitting the sheep with the underside of the cabin and throwing some of them twenty feet into the air. These sheep were someone's livelihood, but this bloke didn't give a stuff. It was an ugly moment.

Some blokes were just plain reckless. Another time, back in Palestine, not long after Tobruk, a few of us decided to head down to Gaza to welcome in the 7th Division, and then go and have a look at the cemetery nearby to pay our respects to the Light Horsemen buried there during World War I. Again, we were picked up by some Australian soldiers in a ute, which was full of lambs bound for an officers' mess in Gaza. I sat in the back with another bloke. The driver took off with a screech of tyres, as if this was Saturday night in Warragul. Down the road he stopped, pulled out a bottle of beer, drank it on his own, then took off again, tyres burning. I didn't like the feel of it at all. Inevitably, there was an accident. The driver said later he had swerved suddenly to avoid a donkey, but I doubt it. We skidded from one side of the road to the other, then through a fence and into a paddock, with the ute tipping over and throwing us all out. My mate Bert Cocks was with the driver in the cabin. He ended up with a bruise the size of a goose egg on his leg — he must have burst a blood vessel or something. No-one broke a limb, but the driver looked to have a broken jaw. We tried to patch him up but we had to abandon him. We didn't have leave passes, and would have been in big trouble if the military police had come along. We scarpered.

This wilful disregard for life and limb was not confined to the Australians, or even a particular type of bloke. When you might be dead tomorrow anyway, no-one gives a stuff.

~

Around March 1942, four others and I, including my friends John Thornton and Curly Leeson, were selected to go to commando school at Aleppo, near the Turkish border. I think my selection must have been based on the desert training we'd been doing in Syria, particularly the night-time desert navigation, which I did pretty well at. For example, you'd be given a compass to go out a mile or so into the desert and then have to find your way back by means of the star formations you could identify and the number of footsteps you'd taken to get out there. But I really wouldn't know what the reasoning was. I didn't ask why; I just did as I was told.

And it was probably a good thing I didn't know what was planned for us; if I had, I mightn't have been too keen to go at all. Much later I discovered that they were trying to gather a mobile corps to make raids behind the German lines, using the Long Range Desert Group and SAS tactics made famous by the Englishman David Stirling. In the desert war, supply lines were long, thin and stretched, and breaking them could have a big impact. Stirling was a little-regarded 'one pipper' — a first lieutenant — when he began this daredevil work, but did his job so well that he became a lieutenant colonel. At one time, his group destroyed 600 German planes on the ground, before they even had a chance to get into the air. But these long-range guerrilla operations were tough and treacherous. I talked about it years later with John Thornton, who became a major. He said it was one thing to reach and blow up targets deep behind enemy lines at night, another to make yourself scarce in the barren landscape the next day. The consequences of being caught were all too obvious. As I said, it was probably a good thing I didn't know any of this then.

At Aleppo we joined a group of British commandos who would train us, and boy was it Wild West stuff. We learned how to jump off buildings, gradually being loaded up with rifles and packs until we could do it in full kit. And then you would be sent into a building with a .45 on each hip to shoot two targets. Until you had knocked the door down, you wouldn't know where the targets were. The idea was to point each foot at a target, then fire along the line of your boot. I never did find out if I hit any of those targets, which is a shame — I'd love to know how I went at that. We also learned how, if a bloke kicked you in the belly while you were lying down, you could catch him, drag him down and knock his head on the concrete. Our teacher for that exercise was a rugged little Scot. 'Kick me, kick me,' he would say, and you would kick him as hard as you could. 'No good, no good,' he would retort. Then he would say, 'Come at me.' So you would, and the next thing you knew, you were flying through the air. There were no mats to land on, of course, just concrete.

About three weeks into the six-week course, I could hardly move. I was sore from climbing over fences, crawling along the ground, and other combat drills. In the last drill we did, half-plugs of gelignite were going off around us as we ran

In Syria, just before being sent to our 'Wild West'
commando camp. That's me in front.

across a stretch of planks. The instructors said they were trying
to make it as real as possible! It was a little silly, that part of it,
and I started to lose a bit of enthusiasm — after being in
Tobruk we didn't really need that type of simulation.

In any case, four weeks into our commando training
course, the El Alamein crisis began to unfold and we were
pulled out to be sent back to our battalion to await orders. The
Allies had had Rommel on the run — the British and Polish

troops who had come in after we left Tobruk had relieved the siege there and chased Rommel all the way back to Benghazi, about 180 miles to the west of Tobruk. But Rommel was not done yet — the previous January he had retaken Benghazi, and by June 21 he recaptured Tobruk. Within a week he was chasing the Allies to El Alamein, near Cairo. He then brought in a dozen 88mm guns, vicious weapons, and in a week destroyed 300 armoured vehicles sent in by the British General Auchinleck at El Alamein. It stalled the Allies there, leaving Egypt in serious danger of complete German invasion.

Rommel, as most know, was clever and cagey; he wasn't called the Desert Fox for nothing. He had set the terms for the desert war. He would, by the ruse of trucks dragging up dust to give the impression he was mobilising his tanks during the day, send his infantry divisions out from the front during the night, into the desert to outflank ours, to attack from behind. This strategy had been impossible at Tobruk, where the harbour's natural fortifications meant that the Allies always kept a toehold. The front for this battle at El Alamein was about twenty-five miles long, running from the Mediterranean in the north to the impassable Qattara Depression in the south. Our best defence would be the countryside itself. In the Qattara Depression, for instance, there was a lot of quicksand, making Rommel's outflanking expeditions hazardous. By the end of July 1942, though, Rommel had just about had enough. When he first arrived in

Africa, his numbers and weaponry were vastly superior to ours, but no longer. At Tobruk we had had no aerial support and not much other help either. It was just us, our rifles, our bayonets and our stubbornness. Now at El Alamein we would have tanks, artillery and, most importantly, planes. It would be a different kind of war altogether.

When we got there, I remember looking up at a dogfight in the skies above the battleground and thinking, this is good. This is real war. It wasn't the technology that excited me so much as the idea that this time we'd be fighting on more equal terms. There must have been about 140,000 of us altogether — Australians, New Zealanders, South Africans, Indians and British — and 120,000 of them — Germans and Italians. Just like a footy match, and this time, on this playing field, it felt like we'd have a fair chance of winning.

7

WHAT THE ARMY WANTS FROM YOU

Tanks, artillery and planes we might have had this time, but they certainly don't make war any easier. The reality was, on our arrival at El Alamein that July, one battalion, the 28th, was lost almost entirely. The 28th was intended to strike a killer blow for the Allied counterattack, get Rommel on the run. I remember waving to a mate of mine from the battalion, Bulla Beams, as they set off into the sunset; he was sitting on the back of a tank waving a bottle of whisky. I don't know what happened to him. Anyway, they were stopped in their tracks, first by a minefield and then by a shell that landed on top of their signal van, blowing their communications to pieces and making their task impossible. Nearly everyone in the battalion was taken prisoner. The result was that both sides dug in along their new lines — a 25-mile-long field of foxholes — and that is pretty much how it stayed until October.

My first night there, I was put in charge of a group of blokes I didn't know — odds and sods, about eight or nine of us — and we all piled around our gear and went to sleep, for our turn would be on in the morning. I got up at 4.30 a.m. and shook them awake, saying, 'You'd better get up. It's going to be on at quarter to five.' I had been forewarned that around that time, as soon as the artillery barrage started, it would be our signal to be off, to join our company at the front line. We had no signal van line or runners for other communications; it was just us and the enemy, and no-one else in our little pocket of the front. The birds had just started chirping their desert morning song, when the artillery opened up and we hopped to it. We hunted around, got a Bren gun out of a box, cleaned the grease off it, dug out some ammunition and put a bloke on the job.

We spread out in battle formation, about twenty yards apart, and away we went — with a slight hold-up. One in my mob was only sixteen years old, poor kid, and he started crying. You can't blame him but I had to yell at him, 'Stop crying or piss off.' He had nowhere else to go; he stopped crying, and came on with us, kept up. But while we were out on that manoeuvre, one of our own planes came across and dropped a bomb right in the middle of us. If that rattled the sixteen-year-

One of the guns of our Australian artillery a 25-pounder — at El Alamein.

old, I wouldn't have known about it; it would've rattled anyone. Fortunately, no-one was hurt. It was a big bomb: when we went back for a look later, the crater was twenty feet wide and four or five feet deep. It must have been dropped to lead the enemy to believe that another wave of infantry was coming in from behind where we were. In any case, the Germans backed off, enabling us to take and stabilise a new position.

We hung onto that front, after that first counterattack, and watched the planes do a lot of the fighting. The planes came over every night, right on sunset. I could never understand why it was always at sunset. I think now that it must have been because it was difficult for our planes to pick out the camouflaged German positions at other times of the day, and that the long shadows of dusk helped. The formation was always eighteen planes. They called it the football team — per the number of players on an Aussie Rules side. Auchinleck had left by this time, and Montgomery had taken over. I think the plane formation was a deliberate calculation on General Montgomery's part, to keep up morale. He was clever in that way. At first we didn't know what to make of him, this British general who'd wear a slouch hat as if to say he understood Australians; and it didn't seem to make sense why, when he'd said the blanket strategy at El Alamein was to 'Kill them or take them prisoner', we were embedded in our sangers again, but he soon turned our heads. Every night, as the planes flew over, we'd say, 'There goes

An Australian taking a moment to write from behind the lines at El Alamein.

Montgomery, bloodying Rommel's nose again.' He did, too. Rommel lost many tanks and his campaign stalled.

But it wasn't all beer and skittles for the pilots. There was a war going on in the sky above us, too. I remember watching one Hurricane fly over without a pilot. I was hoping he'd bailed out. The plane was upside down and low, but still flying, and we could hear the engine ticking over, while behind it came the chatter of machine-gun fire. One night, we watched a twin-engine Boston bomber come back from a sortie alone, looping the loop three or four times above us. I think the plane must have had bombs stuck in its bays, meaning that the pilot could neither drop the bombs nor land again, since that would set them off. He must have taken a hit, because I heard later that a set of bloodied headgear was jettisoned, followed by a parachutist, probably the navigator. I heard that the pilot ditched the plane and its bombs in the ocean, a suicide mission. He was a South African. And you'd never know whose decision was the toughest: the pilot, going to his death, or his mate, having to bail out on him, to live to fight another day.

On the ground, at the end of August, we were joined by a division of Highlanders, the 51st, Scottish lads who'd come to us from England, at the end of August. The 51st Highlanders had largely been lost during the British evacuation at Dunkirk, just before France surrendered to Germany, so these were all new blokes. They were unusual in our midst, too, because El Alamein was almost completely a colonial show,

Aussies having a smoke behind the lines — typically underdressed for the occasion.

apart from two or three English divisions at the Qattara Depression end of the front in the south. We were up in the very north, at the Mediterranean end of the front, and the Highlanders were put between us and the New Zealanders to gain some desert battle experience and confidence, in preparation for our next big counterattack.

As part of this strategy, small groups of Highlanders — say, three or four officers, three or four NCOs and half a dozen privates — were sent out to work with each of the Australian and New Zealand battalions. They would go on patrol with us, to learn the lie of the land and all our tricks. At first we were told we might need some time to get accustomed to each other's language, but we didn't need any

AWM 041926

This is the second defence line behind the front at El Alamein. You can get a sense from this picture how desolate the landscape was — fighting over a piece of wasteland.

such thing — we quickly got on well. They did find us unusual, with our lax attention to the hierarchy of army and our general disregard for uniforms — it's hot, so why wouldn't you cut your trousers down to make shorts? The New Zealanders were a much more civilised and disciplined lot than us apparently — I'd hear one day that Rommel had said he thought the Kiwis the finest soldiers, and if given the choice, he'd only take one Australian battalion into his own, and only use them as attack dogs, because we were too unruly and aggressive for him! Anyway, the Scots liked us for our generosity, too. They and the English survived on minute rations compared with ours, and we would send them back to their own battalions with a big sandbag full of herrings in tomato sauce and bully beef. We were growing sick of herrings in tomato sauce anyway. They're quite nice, you can still get them at the supermarket today, but you'd get sick of roast lamb if you had to eat it every day. The Scots must have liked us quite a lot, actually, because they all said that when they returned to the UK, they would sign off and try to transfer to the 9th Division of the AIF, to rejoin us. Of course they couldn't — transfers between armies weren't allowed — but it's the thought that counts.

The officers among them were curiosities to us, though. They would go apoplectic at us when we boiled a billy in the afternoon, because the Germans were only a mile or so away, on a rise called Ruined Ridge, and the officers were petrified that the smoke from our fires would identify our positions. Some officer would say in a plummy voice, 'You'd better put that fire out, soldier!'

We'd reply, 'It's okay, officer, when the shells land, they'll put the fire out all right.' We were pretty certain the Germans knew where we were anyway. They'd established a strong position for themselves and so had we. There aren't many secrets in war.

During this time, I was also put to work with my mates Curly Leeson and John Thornton and the rest from our commando unit, to keep us together a bit, I think, because the powers that be didn't know whether or not they'd want to use our skills. We were deployed in picking up and salvaging empty shells. It wasn't very dangerous work, but essential, to clear the area of unexploded artillery, and to collect empty shell cases for reconditioning or melting down for new shell cases.

It was nothing compared to the collecting mission I was sent on when we'd first arrived at El Alamein. A month earlier, in July, after the first big counterattack on the 17th, two others and I were sent out to search for the missing men from a company that could not account for all its troops. We found three of them at a place called the Hill of Jesus. They had been dead for a week and were covered in flies, a terrible sight. Somehow, I coped with it. Maybe it was my training as a butcher; I don't know. I said to the two other guys with me,

'How about we take one each?' They didn't answer. They cleared out — literally; they ran away. I could have reported them and had them court-martialled, but I realised that they had been in that counterattack. I didn't know them, but I knew that they had had enough. I thought to myself, how would it help, sending them to jail? I never saw them again, don't know what happened to them. I identified the dead from their meat-tags, walked back on my own to report the location of the corpses, and no-one asked me where my privates were.

But it was on that same lone walk back that I think I realised something had hardened in me, or I'd become detached from what was going on. From the very first, I'd never feared bullets or artillery shells — for the latter, like a machine myself, I would flatten myself on the ground and wait for the dust to settle. Then I'd get up, and walk on. I wouldn't run: that would attract attention. But this time, at the scream of the shell, I dropped to the ground as usual, and then I watched the shell skidding over the side of the hill and bouncing towards me, turning end over end, and all I thought was, this is the first time I've seen a live shell. It didn't explode. Lucky me.

That detachment, that coolness, is exactly what the army wants from you. During our initial desert training, way back at Marsa Matruh, when we were green, before Tobruk, we were being tested for it, being trained to overcome fear. One pitch-black night, we were sent out on a mock patrol and our instruction was to head out into the dark on a certain compass bearing, where eventually we would find a burning lantern, with a guard nearby. Our orders were to get to the lantern and put the light out without the guard ever knowing. We got to within kicking distance of that lantern and spent five minutes or so looking around, steeling ourselves for the task, like the kids we were. Eventually, I said, 'I'm not going to sit here all night. I'm going to put that damn light out.' And that was what I did.

A job like that was about keeping your head and just doing it, just going with whatever comes next. There is no room for such a thing as fear. As I've said, when it comes to the real thing, the adrenalin takes your brain into another gear altogether.

Out in battle, things speed up and slow down at the same time, so that while you're moving and there's who knows what going on around you, you can see and sense in a way that you can't ordinarily. One night, at El Alamein, when I was at the rear of my platoon, being the bloke between us and another platoon coming up behind, ahead of a creeping artillery barrage, we were advancing across German diggings, and I thought to myself, this looks like freshly dug dirt. I took it in at a glance, under the flash artillery fire. It was all going off around us, but I thought, I should have a look at what's going on here. I did and found three German sappers, unarmed field engineers in their white overalls, crouching in the dirt. They looked like three giant frogs, splayed out one behind the other. I gave the head frog a dig in the shoulder with my bayonet and said, '*Hände hoch, hände hoch*!' Hands up, hands up, as we'd been drilled to say. Suddenly, the three of them took off like the Marx brothers into the night, towards our lines. I was yelling out: 'Stop! Halt!' not knowing how to say in German, 'You're going to get killed, you idiots!' I couldn't run after them because I might have run into our own fire. I couldn't shoot them myself because they were unarmed — they were there to dig holes, not fight. Besides, if I had shot at them I might have ended up shooting some of my mates. So I fired a shot into the ground and yelled, 'Prisoners coming up — look out!'

Rommel, the Desert Fox.

The perverse thing about war is that it does have rules, and in the desert both sides observed them. Rommel was a famously fair general. He said the fight had to be hard, but fair and square, like a football match, and it was. That especially meant no shooting prisoners and no shooting unarmed men. All along the front the Australians knew this about Rommel. Not everyone on the German side believed in Rommel's ways. The Schutzstaffel, the infamous SS, detested him, figuring that in war the end justifies any means. But he was staunch; a military man through and through, no interest in politics or the ideologies of his government. We also were scrupulous about obeying the rules. War is hell, and life in war is cheap, but weird as it might seem, there was respect between the sides. We were all soldiers. I know that the rules of engagement were not so closely followed on other fronts in World War II, but they were at El Alamein.

~

It wasn't a bullet or shell or a plane or a tank that was nearly the death of me there, however — it was petrol. That day is burned into my memory.

I was out with the salvage crew, picking up shells and other useful detritus, when an Italian spotter plane, a flimsy little thing like a Tiger Moth, was shot down by our anti-

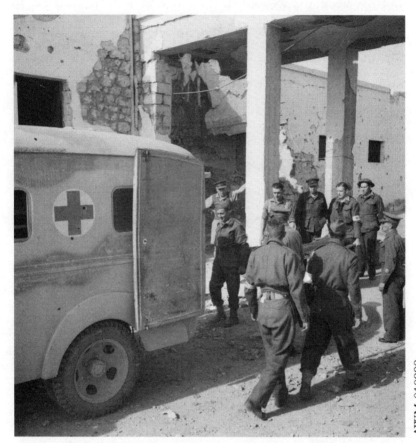

An ambulance making a deposit at the Australian General Hospital, Suez.
I was too crook on my second visit there to notice the trip.

aircraft guns. It flipped, turned a somersault in the air, then crashed into the ground. We were nearby, so we scrambled to the plane and pulled the pilot out. He had been knocked out and his head was bloodied, but he wasn't dead; he'd be all right. Our officer set to souveniring straight away, grabbing a big oil compass out of the plane — he still has it: I saw him many years later one Anzac Day and asked him. But that day, he pulled a silk parachute out of the plane, too, and even though privates and NCOs couldn't hide such loot as officers could, because our kits were searched regularly, he said to me, 'You can have this.' All right, thank you, I thought, and started marching back to my dugout with this silk parachute. I was getting thirsty, and as I went past another dugout near mine, I saw a jerry can sitting on top of it. I felt it. It was nice and cool: water. There were some blokes in the dugout playing pontoon, so I asked them to throw me up a mug. Sure enough, up came a mug. There was no colour in petrol then, and since a wind was blowing off the Mediterranean, I couldn't smell anything. Ah, beautiful water, I thought, and I had poured half a cup of it down my guts before I woke up to what it was.

I ended up with yellow jaundice. The petrol went down through my liver, and the lead in it basically shut that essential organ down and I shut down with it. They put me on a stretcher and sent me down to the Australian General Hospital, Suez Canal. I was so crook that when they brought around a beautiful breakfast the next morning — sausages and bacon — I couldn't eat it. 'Take it away,' I moaned. I was ready to die. Then a nurse came in and offered me a cup of cocoa. 'No,' I said, 'I just want to die.' I meant it. I was twenty-two and I wanted to die, I was that crook.

Eventually, they got me going again with cocoa and meals of steamed chicken and fish. I couldn't have any fats because my liver couldn't take them. I was in hospital for more than two weeks. Gradually I came good, and I have to say I was bloody lucky. It's amazing that I've suffered no ill effects from it since. When I was right again, it was time to go back to war, back to El Alamein.

Out of hospital, I was sent as a supernumerary to another company. We were digging what we thought were new positions, but in fact were preparations for the start of the last big attack on Rommel. One day, while we were labouring away, we noticed a Hurricane fly over, barely a hundred feet above us. On his tail was a German fighter plane and behind him were two more. We let go at them with everything we had, but it was useless. As soon as the Hurricane was over our lines, the Germans shot him down. What had happened was that they had brought him back to die behind his own lines. It was a weird kind of courtesy.

Another day, we watched as a German fighter plane came down and belly-landed on the road, then stared in amazement as the pilot — a little bloke — got out, took a mirror out of

Corbis SF37818

Aussies taking a breather in the desert.

his tunic pocket and combed his hair before walking over to us to surrender, cheeky as you like. His plane was a new model, not seen by us much before, and immediately the authorities ran a roll of barbed wire around it to stop anyone getting in to take a look before a truck could arrive to tow it back to base quickly — so that another fighter wouldn't get the chance to fly over and blow it up. But it was that cheeky little pilot who made the greater impression on me.

Maybe being Australian I appreciated his attitude, as cheek was part of our character, too — in any and every circumstance. Even when Winston Churchill came to visit us at El Alamein. Of course, it was something of a highlight. One battalion, the 24th, lined up along the road to welcome him, and there was plenty of genuine cheering for him, and respect. We knew it was Churchill who was holding Britain's war effort together with his skill as a statesman, keeping the British people staunch. In the typical Australian way, one of our blokes yelled out, 'What about a cigar, Winnie?' And Churchill, who knew plenty about cheek himself, stopped and gave him one.

A movie moment perhaps. But there were plenty of them in the extreme conditions that war brings, many of them involving feats of improbable heroism. Only a handful of them end up in movies or books. One occasion that comes to mind for me is the night at El Alamein that I got talking to a tall, blond Digger. Sadly, I didn't ask his name or battalion, and I still don't know it. 'It's good to be back,' he said by way of introduction to his story. He had been taken prisoner at El Alamein in July 1942, at the beginning of the campaign, but later escaped and undertook a solo trek of perhaps 500 miles to get back to us. He said the hardest aspect of his flight was not heat or hunger, or the thought that he might at any moment be recaptured. It was the loneliness. He had managed to get hold of an Italian uniform, and sometimes passed himself off to the Germans as an Italian, pleading the language barrier with hand gestures. In this way, he was able to scrounge water and food. But that did not constitute human company as such. At nights, he would sneak as close as he dared to German camps, just to hear them talking. It was risky, he said, but it saved his sanity.

As I listened to him, I thought, yes, there's nothing more lonely on earth than a human on his or her own. As an old man now, I know it as the truth. I wake up at nights and think, Godfather, I'm on my own. It's almost frightening. But back then I was never alone.

All that digging my mates and I had spent weeks doing at El Alamein — without knowing why, of course — turned out to be for weapons pits for what would become one of the most important battles of the war — the battle that would lead eventually to the finish for Rommel in Africa. About a week before it was due to start, I was transferred to another company. My new job was to go out with some others a mile and half or so in front of our lines, deliberately drawing German fire. As at Tobruk, the point of the exercise was for our officer to get a bearing on enemy positions and strength. So out we would go, half-crouching, half-running, until the bullets began to whistle over our heads, then we'd pull back, never getting close enough for them to 'crack' in your ear as they whizzed by.

In this fashion, we worked our way along the front. Captain Walker, our officer, had his compass out, making notes and taking bearings. At one point we came across a big pile of 44-gallon petrol drums, several dozen stacked about twenty feet high, lining both sides of a road, and Captain Walker despatched me to see if anyone was hiding among them. Despite what I said earlier about detachment, it was nerve-racking, advancing on that silent menace. I walked across the front of the nearest pile — at least there I was covered from behind, I hoped — then worked my way around and back through the middle. I found no-one. But it might have been a listening post. We knew the Germans were not stupid. If there was a bloke hiding in one of those drums, on surveillance, he was very quiet — like me, he would've been holding his breath.

Finally, all was ready. The attack was scheduled to begin at 9.40 p.m. on October 23, and we were only told the day before. The idea was to try to punch a hole far into Rommel's defences, which were about ten miles deep, and isolate a

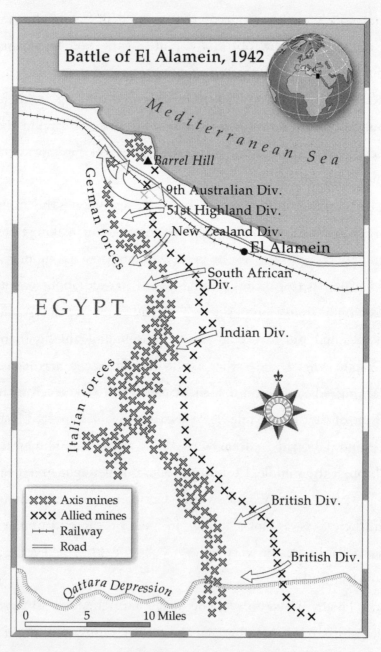

Battle of El Alamein, 1942

Mediterranean Sea

▲ Barrel Hill

× 9th Australian Div.

51st Highland Div.

New Zealand Div.

● El Alamein

South African Div.

German forces

Italian forces

EGYPT

Indian Div.

×××	Axis mines
×××	Allied mines
┼┼┼	Railway
───	Road

British Div.

British Div.

Qattara Depression

0   5   10 Miles

Montgomery's Allied offensive in October 1942 involved cutting the Italian forces off from the Germans. We were attacking to the north.

strategically vital strip of coast where the road and railway ran. It was a place we called the Saucer, as it lay on low ground between the railway embankment and the embankment of the road, and we were to draw the Germans towards us there and hold that front. If successful, it would also divide the Germans from the Italians, and ultimately stop the Axis forces from gaining their objective: getting around us and making for Alexandria, only sixty miles to the east, to fuel, food and a firm base in North Africa.

Twelve hundred artillery guns sounded the beginning of the battle, pounding the Germans as our tanks and engineers came in, clearing the minefields and cutting into the German front about seven miles deep and five miles wide, with us infantry coming in behind. We stabilised our positions and then, on the night of October 30 at 11 p.m., we charged again, and us infantry made a hell of a racket ourselves. 'Ho, ho, ho,' we shouted, as if we were on a kangaroo shoot. Unruly and aggressive, probably, but it was our way of keeping our spirits up, urging each other on. That battle would last twelve hours, until ten o'clock the next morning, when word came back that the Allies' strategy had worked, exactly as predicted by Montgomery.

The actual fighting went on for ten days in total, from that first night of the 23rd. General Montgomery had figured that the Germans would defend that piece of coast with all their might, and they did. It was pretty bloody. One night I came across half a German, lying on the ground. His legs had been blown away; he had probably taken a direct hit from a 25-pounder shell. It wasn't a pretty sight. I got him into a nearby dugout. He was the first dead German I had seen. But I didn't flinch, inwardly or outwardly. As I walked past him, I felt no more emotion than I might have if I'd come across a dead bullock in a paddock back home. It might sound callous but war doesn't leave any room for sentiment. Sometimes, it is only later in life, much later, that the full horror hits home.

I witnessed another German die that same night. He had got lost in the fighting, and was seriously wounded. We could hear him groaning, alone in the dark, but it was too dangerous to try to set foot out there. Eventually, one of the Bren gunners fired a round in his direction. After that, we heard no more. We found him the next morning, dead on the ground in front of us. We rooted through his pockets and found photographs of his family, his kids, his pet dog. It was the same sort of stuff our blokes carried around in their pockets. We were fighting ordinary men, just like us. That's the foolishness of war.

But even still, within it all, there were moments of pleasure. On what would prove to be my last night at El Alamein, some others I knew found a sack of potatoes in the hold of an abandoned German tank. It was like finding hidden treasure. Gleefully, they cooked them up quick smart, but just as they were about to eat, one in their company clutched his stomach, groaned and nearly passed out. They pulled up his shirt and found a big hole in his stomach, made by a bullet. Either he hadn't known about it or had been trying to hide it. A signals bloke came along, saw the damage and asked, 'Got a pair of pliers?' Someone did, and the sig bloke pulled the bullet out as casually as if he was pulling out a bent nail. That wounded soldier was lucky. The bullet had somehow lodged in the soft tissue of his belly, when it probably should have ripped right through him. Thus was a life saved; something to feel pleased about, for a moment.

8
BROUGH LOSES TODAY

That same night, we drove the Germans back a bit more and I took six prisoners. The next morning, we searched their dugouts. Just as I came across what had been their headquarters, in a pit six or seven feet deep, I saw a curtain — a camouflage sheet — move. '*Hände hoch!*' I yelled. 'Hands up. Come on out.' Out peeped a face, then the German soldier it belonged to emerged and slowly climbed up the steps. His right foot was badly smashed up, possibly having been mangled by a shell. We were wary of him at first, of course, as he could have had a grenade on him or who knows, but it became quickly clear he wasn't much interested in doing anything. So, we gave him a cigarette and sat him down.

Then there was a race to get down into the dugouts, where we found another treasure trove. In the first dugout there were German grenades, a sandbag full of Lugers, half a dozen Sten guns — compact submachine guns that fold up, like Tommy guns — a box of 90mm ammunition and a big set of binoculars that could see nearly ten miles away. Our officer, Jack Frost, pocketed those binoculars. There were coloured pencils, too, even a colour camera, made with beautiful German precision. We also found a leather case on the wall. In it was a map of the entire Russian front, from the Baltic to the Crimea. A red line marked all the territory the Germans had won. I thought, that will do me, and claimed it as a souvenir. In another abandoned dugout, we found a heap of preserved pears — Italian whole pears — and we devoured them on the spot. We were all set up with a sandbag of guns to cart back to our lines. Everybody in our party would end up with an automatic weapon. It was the loot of momentary victory.

But before we carted off our hoard we had to decide what to do with the wounded German. When I asked Jack Frost, he said, 'Do whatever you like, but he's going to need treatment, isn't he?' On that foot, yes. We could have taken him back to our own unit, near the railway line, but that was about 400 yards away. A little nearer, about 300 yards away, was a big Red Cross tent, set up in no-man's-land, on what had been German territory — the place would be full of Germans. I pointed to it and gestured to the soldier as if to say, 'How about there?' He didn't reply. So I lifted him up and put him on my back.

There was one of those vicious 88mm guns manned by the Germans on a hill nearby and it put a few bursts past us as we set off. Amazing machines, they were, with a missile designed to burst in the air about twenty feet up, sending out a great black plume of smoke with a tongue of flame about ten feet long and a savage shower of ball-bearing shrapnel. As it fired it would make a sound like a thunderclap, and the shell burst had an ear-splitting crack to it. At first, it didn't worry me. I had the little camera I'd souvenired with me, and started taking photos of the gun. Unbelievable! Geez, I must have been mad at that moment. There I was with a bloke on my back, looking at this machine and its black smoke, thinking, this'd make a good photo! Of course, I lost the camera — only a couple of hours later, as it would turn out. But just then, another shell thundered out and came so close I stumbled and fell over, right on top of the German's foot. I was more worried about him than me — his foot really was a terrible mess. I bet that's hurting, I thought. I was a bit shaken, too — well, a lot really. But I couldn't let him see that I was frightened — *wouldn't* let him have the satisfaction of that, I suppose. He wasn't saying anything.

I picked him up and started walking again. Another shell roared by and exploded about fifty yards behind us. I just kept walking, straight towards the aid post. I figured the Germans must have known by then that if they got me, they would be taking out one of their own, too. Or maybe the bloke on my back signalled to them; I'd never know. If there was a way, I'd love to get in touch with that German soldier and ask him. Boy, would we have a chat about that day! As it happened, the Germans didn't fire another shot at us.

I walked right up to the tent and pulled out my stolen Luger. One of their officers came out and made a gesture as if to say, 'Don't get too aggressive.'

I said, 'Here's your bloke.' I put him down, turned around and began to walk back. My mind was racing. I thought, do I run? Do I crawl? What do I do? In the end, I decided that I would bloody well walk all the way back, with my backside to the enemy. And I did, as if I owned the place, hoping my confidence would rub it in for those watching. I bet it did. They were, after all, losing to these Aussie attack dogs. And no-one fired a single shot.

~

It was only an hour or two after my mercy mission that things in our pocket of the war began to go wrong. It was early morning now and we could see the German tanks mobilising at a place called Barrel Hill. We tried to get word back to our artillery to fire on them, but we couldn't make contact. Our

One of Rommel's vicious 88mm guns.
This one has been captured by the men of my battalion.

runner made two or three dashes to try to find the artillery officer, but couldn't locate him. The German tanks, four of them abreast, had moved to within a hundred yards of us and were belting into us with shells and machine guns. We were supposed to have six anti-tank guns with us, but they hadn't been able to get over the steep railway embankment the previous night. Our engineers ended up blowing a hole under the railway line with anti-tank mines to get them through, but it was too late for us.

Eventually, our artillery opened up on the German tanks, but it was already over. We reached the point where there were the four German tanks in front of us and one looming from behind. We were in our sangers with nowhere to go. We were trapped. If we didn't do something we were at risk of being run over and buried by the tanks — it wasn't unknown for them to twist back and forth over their tracks on top of a foxhole, effectively screwing soldiers into the ground. You wouldn't want to die that way. 'What are you going to do?' I asked our commanding officer.

'Looks like we'll have to pack it in,' he replied flatly.

So the ignominious moment came and I had to put my hands up in the age-old gesture of surrender. All sixteen of us caught there did. Thankfully, the tanks backed off, their guns still trained on us. It was October 31, 1942, and my war, as far as combat went, was over. It was a dreadful feeling — sad and humiliating — to just have to stop. Drop everything, it's

This is a German tank knocked out by Allied artillery. It's a pity that those in our area didn't meet the same fate before surrounding us, forcing our surrender.

finished. And we did have to drop our stolen loot immediately, as according to the 'rules' you couldn't be in possession of enemy equipment or uniforms. Winston Churchill's own son was almost shot for wearing a German cap when captured, because according to these rules he could be seen to be impersonating a German soldier and therefore accused of being a spy. He wasn't shot, of course. Rommel was a long way from stupid. Shooting the British PM's son would have brought a huge amount of focus to his North African campaign and possibly a very swift and brutal halt to it. But for us, for me, halt it was. Not brutal, but swift and very tough to swallow.

We were moved behind enemy lines across to some sand dunes towards the beach. All the while our artillery was sending shells over, trying to give us a chance to make a break, I guess. Sand was blasting up all around us but there was nowhere to go. As I stood there in the dunes, a German officer came along and said, 'How old are you?'

I said, 'Twenty-two.'

'You're a bit young to be a sergeant, aren't you?' he asked.

I said, 'No, we've got plenty my age — we've got officers only twenty-one.' That was true. I was due to go to officer school in Cairo when this stunt was over, and had been in the position of acting lieutenant just prior to this. If I hadn't been captured, I would have come home a lieutenant. I wasn't thinking about that then, though: I wasn't thinking about anything other than where I was, and focusing on the German officer speaking to me.

He looked thoughtful for a moment, then he asked, 'Why do you Australians volunteer for war? You must like it.' He understood that we were a long way from home, but so was he, and maybe he was thinking about that.

I replied, 'We don't like war. We're just here to get you guys to go home so that we can go home.'

Then, like I needed the fact rubbed in, he said, with his rubbery old German accent, 'For you, the war is over.'

I was searched then by some other guy, looking for revolvers under my arms, extra weapons and so on. I just copped it: Brough loses today, bad luck. Nothing I could do about it. He took a bit of money off me, three Egyptian pounds — that irked me — but nothing else. As soon as I knew I was about to be taken prisoner, I'd smashed my watch. I'd bought the watch in Tel Aviv, to replace the one that went walkabout at Tobruk, and it was a fine watch. I wasn't going to give them anything of value. I suppose that in my mind I had already started trying to escape. They weren't really going to take me and keep a hold of me, not that I had any idea of how I was going to get away. I didn't know it at the time, but one of our party already had made off: a stocky little bloke called Dubba Doughton had snuck off in the confusion as the tanks came in, and he snaffled my camera on his way out, as I'd be told, many years later. Still not sure what irks me more

— that he took off on his own or that he pinched my pictures of that damn gun!

But now I had nothing except the clothes on my back, and I was all fired up to give the Germans nothing in the way of information either. To my surprise, though, I wasn't interrogated. I couldn't believe it. I can only think that word had gotten around about my rescue of the German soldier earlier. Everyone else who was captured that day was called in for questioning. Under the 'rules' all they had to disclose was their name, number and rank, but who knows what was said. I do know that when we were piled into a truck afterwards for the night, half the blokes began talking about what had happened and about their mates — the who and where and what and how — until I said, 'Will you bloody well shut up.' As if the Germans weren't listening and taking note of every word they said.

But it wouldn't have mattered anyway. Within days, the Germans were gone from El Alamein. They mounted twenty counterattacks in the two days after we were caught, assailing the Australians while they were trying to get their own troops out and back along the coast to Benghazi in the west. They lost nearly two hundred men and it was all over for them. By then, I was on the move myself: in a prison truck on the way to Tripoli — the one in Libya held by the Italians.

~

It was an eventful journey which would take about ten days. Along the way I looked out from the truck at miles of gum trees, imported from Australia because they grow well in a hot, dry climate. The sight of them made me homesick, made me think of all those blokes who'd been shipped back home on what I thought of as the Pineapple Train, to fight in the Pacific. Of course I didn't know what they were copping by that time, but looking at those eucalypts, so far from home themselves, I decided to escape straight away. There were probably about thirty of us in that truck, and I put word around that if any of them felt like it, we could knock off the guards and head south. I knew the push was coming, that the Germans were on the run and that they wouldn't bother to chase us. There were only two guards on the truck and a driver, all Italians — because all prisoners taken by the Axis forces in North Africa, regardless of who captured them, were given over to the Italians. We could have overwhelmed them and taken control easily. But the other blokes didn't want to be in it. I guess they had had enough.

One bloke, a fellow I knew called Sandy Harvey, showed the general mood. He was looking over the side of the truck, a few days into the trip, when one of the guards decided to touch him on the arse with his bayonet. Sandy went berserk. He jumped up, snatched the rifle away from the Italian and said, 'I'm going to shoot you, you little bastard.' He meant it. He could have killed the bugger there and then; he had the rifle in his hands. But he changed his mind, threw the gun back to the guard and said, 'Don't do that again.' There was a mix of that twitchiness and exhaustion among us; we were too battle-weary and defeated to make a proper go of escape but still full of fire. And I couldn't do it on my own, not in that terrain, not in the state I was in.

At night the truck would stop and we'd be herded out and put behind wire with a machine gun trained on us. We passed through Bardia, and then Tobruk, and then at a stop at Benghazi we saw a big prisoner-of-war camp, full of Australians. They'd been there since July, and they were in a far worse state than we were. It looked like they were being starved. It was pitiful. But we were moved on again, and we weren't being starved — not quite. The rations were meagre: the Italians would give us a tin of about 250 grams of bully beef and an Italian biscuit, about five inches square and an inch thick. I don't know what it was made of, but it had the consistency of cement. It was so hard that you couldn't really eat it, but had to suck on it. It would take you all day to finish. Some of the guys cut picture frames out of them! I had a better idea, one I'd learned from reading about how the Diggers had managed in World War I: I would save my biscuit and beef until the end of the day, then I'd pull the lining out of my tin hat and use the hat as a saucepan. I'd smash the biscuit on a rock, put it and the beef into the helmet, add a bit of water, find some sticks on the roadside, put a match to them and boil up a kind of stew. Then my tin hat would be warm, too, for when I went to sleep. I did this all the way to Tripoli.

When we got to Tripoli, we were loaded into the hold of a coastal freighter, bound for Italy. Only a short trip, north across the Mediterranean from Libya and through the Strait of Messina around Sicily, but we were all worried that we might be torpedoed by British submarines, with good reason. We'd heard on the grapevine that it had happened to another prison boat, costing about thirty Allied lives. So we decided we would sing all night, as loudly as we could. We sang every song we knew, beginning with 'Pack Up Your Troubles In Your Old Kitbag' and 'Roll Out the Barrel', then sang them all again. Years later I asked a navy mate of mine, Henry Pegrum, about our ploy. Henry was president of our Rats of Tobruk club, and he said we probably would have been heard three miles away under water. The Italians must have wondered what the hell was going on. They kept telling us to shut up; what they didn't realise is that we were saving their souls as well as ours. It worked. We made it to Italy alive.

9
LOCKED DOWN

We must have been a pathetic sight as we were unloaded at Reggio Calabria on the toe of Italy's boot and were marched through the streets. It was now about two weeks since we'd been captured. We hadn't had a wash, nor had enough to eat. I should have weighed about twelve stone at the time, but was down to about ten and a half; I also had a great big sore on my backside from rattling around on the hard boards of that truck across Libya. In the streets, the Italians stared at us. 'Look at the English, the poor English,' they said. 'How do they expect to win the war?' A lady gave me an orange as we went by, and I don't know if I thanked her, but I appreciated that small kindness very much. I kept that orange until we got onto the train, then split it into eleven pieces, for the eleven

AWM P02793.003

The administrative section of Italian prison camp PG57. The grim look
on the sentry's face might suggest the *carabinieri* who guarded the place
didn't much like their work — or us.

of us crammed into the compartment, so we all had a bit. It was our only ration.

I don't know how many prisoners there were on that train but there must have been quite a few, if us eleven were sharing just two seats. It was bloody uncomfortable but by then we were past caring. There was no toilet. I still had a touch of dysentery, so I had to poke my backside out a window while the other blokes hung onto me and do my business that way. It didn't matter to me that people were looking straight at my bum. I'd lost my manners as regards such things in North Africa. There was no place or use for dignity here or there.

The train took us north, past Mount Vesuvius, glowing in the dark, past Naples, and after about eight hours straight up, almost to Trieste in the north-east, to a place called Udine, between the Italian Alps and the border with Slovenia — not that we knew where we'd arrived at the time. There, we were taken to a camp called PG57, near a village called Gruppignano. The PG in PG57 stood for *Prigioniero di Guerra*, prisoner of war, and this was a camp for them all right. It was a large complex of detention centres, for Australians, New Zealanders, Indians and British, probably about two or three thousand men in all — and several billion lice as well. Our huts in the Australian part were like big wooden barns, sleeping thirty or forty to a hut in double bunks with two men up, two men down, and with a small heater in the middle. Not too bad as digs in themselves, but this would be home for nearly the next ten months, including all of a long winter.

It was a bugger of a time, and the first two or three months through that winter were the worst for me. I lost my way a bit, got pretty down, being locked down, and any thought of escape left me. The weather didn't help. It would snow, then it would rain, then the ground would freeze over at night. It made simply getting around hazardous, like walking on glass, arms and legs all over the place. It was that cold the skin on your toes would callus. The camp was full, too, and that made the Italians nervous and frightened. They had a guard posted every 100 metres around the perimeter of the camp. You could hear them during the night, stamping their feet against the cold and calling out to one another: '*Io, Io.*' Me, Me. I guess they were trying to reassure each other. 'Freeze to death, you bastards,' we would mutter to ourselves.

And they *were* bastards, these Italians. There had been an escape from PG57 not long before we arrived — two other blokes from Drouin, Howard Phillips and Ted Higgs, who was a couple of years younger than me and used to ride a horse to school, too, had been involved in the breakout. It had been raining for three weeks and the camp was awash. Nineteen of them dug a tunnel and crawled through it one night. They said they had a boat waiting somewhere on the coast over the Slovenian border. But getting out was one thing; getting away was another. The Italians rounded them all up, and when they brought them back into the camp, they shaved the escapees' heads and then chained them to a pole in the middle of the special detention section — for three weeks. War is a cruel business, but I have to say that the Italians were cruel beyond the pale. There was no rhyme or reason to their actions or punishments. Every morning, they would line us up for inspection, and if they didn't like the look of you, they would point and say, 'You.' Then you'd be taken off to the 'boob' — solitary confinement — for twenty-eight days. Bread and water only, no cigarettes, no company. I managed to avoid it. I worked out that if you didn't look them in the eye it was less likely that they would take a dislike to you. So I would look up at the sky. It was all I *could* do. As a POW, you had no rights, there was no way to question or complain about your treatment. And that got to me, badly.

They treated us like criminals rather than prisoners of war. If there'd been some kind of soldierly respect or understanding between us and the Germans, there was none with the Italians. Our jailers were *carabinieri*, military police, but they didn't seem to have any rules about their business. Some of our blokes would stage concerts in the NCOs' hut to amuse themselves. They would dress up, make costumes from bits and pieces of this and that, sing vaudeville songs, all very 'gay', and making a racket, and that seemed to be fine with the guards. I never went to one of these concerts, but

The prison huts at PG57. The resentment and anger returns like it was yesterday just looking at them.

one night I heard a bunch of them singing a song called 'The Whitehorse Inn', just singing a silly song, and one of the *carabinieri* came in and said in an accusing tone, 'You're singing "God Save the King".' They weren't, of course, but it broke the party up. A little while later the same officer came to our hut and said to the bloke who was sharing my bunk — Clive Loney — who'd been at the concert, 'You! Come!' Clive had to spend twenty-eight days in the boob, and he hadn't done a bloody thing.

These Italians were nervous, jumpy; they were never at ease. Even our religious observance was a drama for them. On Sundays they would hold a church parade in the camp and bring in a priest to give a sermon and say prayers. But they made sure there was a guard with a machine gun at each corner of the compound. Christianity at the muzzle of a machine gun. How ridiculous was that! I only turned up once; couldn't take it. I'd been a Sunday school goer as a kid — under the influence of my mum's Methodism — and I'd even once thought that I might like to be a missionary in New Guinea when I grew up. But I'd drifted from it as I got older, and then the war seemed to take whatever was left of it. The Germans wore belt buckles that said, '*Gott Mit Uns*', God with Us, while we'd sung 'Onward Christian Soldiers' before belting into each other; and now the Italians were delivering God to the unarmed and half-starved under threat of death. I walked away, thinking, shoot me if you want to, mongrels;

and they might have if the mood took them, because their skittishness did make them trigger-happy.

There was a bloke in the camp called 'Sock' Symonds who'd illustrate this aspect of the *carabinieri*'s character for us very sharply. Symonds had been with us at Tobruk. His company made an attack on some high ground there one day but suffered so many casualties that they couldn't hold it. The next day they arranged a truce with the Germans so that both sides could pick up their dead and wounded. Sock was acting as a stretcher-bearer when he found a dead German wearing a beautiful watch. He unstrapped it and pocketed it; the trouble was that a German officer saw him. 'It's against the rules to rob the dead,' the German said. 'You are now my prisoner.' So Symonds ended up in PG57 long before us. But he would never make it out.

Trouble for him in the camp came one day during a baseball match in the compound. There'd been some home-brew grog going round that day. Just as the blokes made their own baseballs and cricket balls out of rocks bound with silver paper and string, some of the guys would get their hands on dried fruit and a little yeast from the canteen, where we could buy such luxuries after saving up the one lire a week — the nothing — we 'earned', and make up a brew. This day Symonds had no doubt had a bit of a tipple. He was making a bit of noise, having a bit of fun. It wasn't unusual for rowdiness during the baseball matches — some blokes would bet their vital Red Cross rations on the outcome of a game. But this day our captors took offence, and six guards came along and began to cart Symonds off to the boob.

I was watching the scene unfold from the back of our hut. A few weeks earlier, I'd spent my saved-up lire on a packet of carrot seeds from the canteen and was trying to grow them in a patch of soil there. I was tending those carrot seedlings as I watched the *carabinieri* with Symonds. He was shouting and swearing, but he wasn't attacking them physically. Suddenly, one of them walked around, raised his gun and shot Symonds dead. Just like that.

It shocked me for a moment. But I didn't lose any sleep over it. You couldn't afford to fret about things like that. In my mind it was another bloke gone, simple as that. That was how I had to think of it. It was just another day. After the war I would read that the colonel who ran that camp was executed for his war crimes, such as shooting unarmed prisoners. I was glad about that. Back then, amidst it all, the only resort I had was to revert to the idea that this was part of the job. As I had in North Africa, I would take each moment as it came, not knowing what was coming round the corner.

Others died in the camp less dramatically — of illness and malnutrition. Illness was rife. For the first few months it was freezing, and the toilet was just a big open trench which was only occasionally drained. The lice, which carry typhus, were incredible: even after washing your clothes and having

A typical Red Cross POW parcel, containing little 'luxuries' for us — such as soap!

them snap freeze as they 'dried', those lice, their tiny bums blue from the cold, would spring back to life as soon as it warmed. It wasn't unusual for our essential Red Cross parcels not to turn up, either, or for the one bread roll allocated to us daily to go missing. '*Pani domani*,' the guards would say — Bread tomorrow. We lived mainly on rice soup, which, if we were lucky, might have a bit of cabbage in it, or a piece of gristle, or a caterpillar or two. If we were really lucky, there'd be macaroni floating in it, and we'd cut open our bread rolls — if we had any — and pull out the soft insides and stuff the macaroni in the crust, toast it on the heater in the hut and pretend we were having a hamburger. Fooling yourself, playing tricks with your own mind, taking pleasure where you can, is part of the deal. It has to be.

I spent my twenty-third birthday — February 16, 1943 — there in PG57, and to celebrate it I made elaborate plans. For about six weeks leading up to the day, I 'rented out' the cheese I got in my Red Cross packages — pieces of matured cheddar about half an inch thick and two inches square. I told the blokes I rented my cheese to that I'd want it back on the 16th. They were as good as their word. On my birthday I received nine pieces of cheese and I sat down and ate the bloody lot.

Those Red Cross parcels really were a lifeline — there'd be powdered milk, coffee, teabags, biscuits, sometimes a bit of honey, sometimes jam. You could count days by the rations you gave yourself: I'll have one biscuit with honey today, and I'll have one biscuit with cheese tomorrow. They delivered not just some extra nutrition but some sanity as well.

The biggest challenge of life in the prison camp was to find ways of passing the days. One of the projects I set myself was to make a suitcase out of old biscuit and jam tins. I cut the rims off the tins, flattened the tins, folded them down about three-eighths of an inch, top and bottom, and slotted the pieces into each other. I had a six-inch nail and a block of wood for a hammer, and I used them to press and strengthen the seams. It was a beautiful piece of work, if I do say so myself — about two feet across and six inches deep, with a handle. Of course, I was never going to have any use for a suitcase in a POW camp. I made it purely for something to do, to take my mind off the helplessness of imprisonment. You had to have such diversions.

I took up chess there, too. You could spend half a day on one game. You would forget about your stomach, soreness, homesickness, everything except the next move. My on-the-job memory training as a delivery boy back in Drouin came to the fore once again for me, and I quickly memorised all the different openings. I became quite good at the game. Chess is terrific. It teaches you so much, in terms of concentration, strategy, and how to constructively waste time. One bloke, a New Zealander called Best, took the memory games to a new level. He'd regularly give these talks where he'd stand up and tell a story, and then at the end of it pick blokes from the audience and ask them to recall this detail and that. Some of the blokes got so good at the game they could recite the tales back to him.

It was the sun, when it finally came out, that helped me the most, I think. Just to sit in the sun, peeling the callused skin off my toes, feeling the warmth sink into my bones. Cheers you up like nothing else. The sun is food for the body as much as it was for my carrots. It made me feel less hungry and stronger. It brought me back to myself in a way.

I never did get to taste those carrots planted behind the hut, though. They still weren't fully grown and ready to be dug up when I left PG57.

10

DEAD HERO OR LIVE COWARD

We woke up one morning in the middle of 1943 to find that things had changed. Italy had capitulated — the government and the people had given up the war games, as Britain and America took Sicily and then made an air raid on Rome, not that we knew any of that at the time. All we knew was that our Italian guards had abandoned the camp, which had suddenly been taken over by the Germans. The new German guards were cool, calm and methodical, unlike the excitable Italians. Instead of a guard every 100 metres, there was one in each corner of the camp, with a machine gun and a searchlight. But the war had changed for them, too, now that they had lost an ally, and within twenty-four hours, they began to ship us out.

We were divided into two trainloads. Selection was completely random. The longer train went to Görlitz, a German–Polish border town, and those on board would be sent to work in the coal mines there. My mates from Drouin, Ted Higgs and Howard Phillips, and a couple of other Gippsland boys were on that train. I ended up on the other train, bound for Austria.

We were put into freight wagons, little cattle trucks, about twenty-five men to a wagon, and the train rattled along all night, getting colder and more uncomfortable by the hour. No toilet of course: just an allocated corner to do your business in. I don't think there was a single bloke not thinking of escape on that whole train. We hopped to our plan straight off, and those of us with pocket knives started cutting into the wall of the windowless wagon, to try to make a hole big enough to get an arm out to unbolt the door from the outside. We didn't succeed in getting the job done before morning brought us to our destination, and with hindsight, I think that was probably a good thing, too. We'd find out later that some of our guys in another wagon did jump the train, after using their knives to loosen and lift the planks of the floor. They waited until the train slowed or stopped, then wriggled out the bottom. But escaping the train was only half the story. They had meant to get to Switzerland — a neutral country — but they didn't know where they were, nor which direction to take. In any case, the surrounding countryside was full of Germans. All but a couple would be caught pretty quickly.

We finished up in a camp called Stalag 18 A/Z, in a place called Spittal, near the River Drau, in southern Austria, again not far from the Slovenian border — and again, not that we knew where the hell we were. Spittal was in a very pretty valley, with a backdrop of rolling mountains. We weren't, of course, in a frame of mind to appreciate it then, but compared with the Italian camp, it was immediately apparent we'd found ourselves in much better circumstances. The huts were smaller, cosier, twelve to a room, and with single triple-stacker bunks. One of the first things we were given were our prisoner-of-war tags — an important detail the Italians had never bothered with. I still have my tag: it's a rectangular piece of lead stamped with the number of the Stalag and my prisoner number — 7610 — on it. It is a reminder of my good fortune. The tag is scored down the middle, and if I had died in the POW camp, the tag would have been broken in half along that line: one half to be buried with me, the other to be sent to the Red Cross with an indication of where I had been buried. Gladly, it never came to that.

The guards here were men simply doing their job, with a minimum of fuss and bother. After those ten months with the Italians, that in itself was a relief. It's not as though you'd have a chat and a smoke with them — most had as little English as we had German anyway — but there was enough understanding between us that we could be a bit cheeky. We'd tell them we were going to win the war, and they'd come back at us telling us to behave ourselves, reminding us that we were prisoners and they were our captors. It was a lot more relaxed. They would take us out a mile or so into the surrounding forest to collect firewood, and on one such occasion we found a field of maize and pinched a few cobs. The guards were only interested in us getting that firewood, not watching every move we made. Near to the compound, about a hundred yards away, there was a farm building, where a couple of us were sent to shell dried French beans, up in the loft of the place. Well, while we were at it we tucked our trousers into our socks and stuffed as many of those beans as we dared down our legs, then took them back to camp, soaked them and cooked them up. Added to the regular Red Cross rations, and the staple at Spittal of heartier potato soup, these petty thefts meant we were never quite as hungry as we had been in Italy. But that bean pulp we cooked up did a job in our bellies, I can tell you — it was great to have a laugh at a few good, healthy farts.

It was just as cold at Stalag 18 A/Z as it had been in PG57, and we had to try to keep the fires going all the time in the huts, for warmth and for heating our food. Firewood was in constant need. There was an old shed inside the compound at Spittal, not used for anything, as it had no roof. Its weatherboards were intact when we arrived, but bit by bit

Stalag 18 A/Z in the Austrian Alps.

they disappeared. You would be in your hut and you would hear the sound of splitting timber as one was peeled away — crash, bang, wallop — and hauled off to a fire somewhere. We stripped it down until just the frame remained. All of a sudden one day, there was a hell of a noise. We looked outside and saw that the whole shed was gone, the frame pulled apart in five minutes. The guards must have wondered what that racket was, but they didn't object or punish anyone.

One who was probably the cheekiest among us was a bloke called Eric Batty. He was a New Zealander, a corporal with the Field Ambulance and a horse-breaker and buckjump rider before he joined up. Eric somehow ended up in my room and told me that before we'd met he'd gone out with another mate, grabbed a couple of mattocks from the garden area of the compound and indicated to the guard on duty by the wire that he'd been told to take down one of the fence posts. The guard bought the story, nodded to them to get on with it. So they did. They pinched that post and chopped it up for firewood. Of course, the post had to be replaced so that part of the wire didn't collapse, and Eric did it as much for the lark of it as for the wood. Just to get away with it. Something to do.

Here in Stalag 18 A/Z, as in PG57, we had to make our own amusements. I kept on with my chess, of course, but some of the blokes were quite ingenious with their tinkering. One lot made their own compasses. They would get a razor blade, unscrew the electric light globes, put the razor blade in the light socket and leave it there all night. The blade would become magnetised. Then they would use a pin to attach the blade to a piece of cardboard, and around and around it would go. In the camp in Italy, some blokes had made their own wind-up fans out of billies, which were all made out of biscuit tins, like my long-lost suitcase. They used the fans in makeshift airshafts to ventilate the tunnels some were digging to escape. Very clever. I didn't see any tunnels myself, but I heard about them, and while I never fancied their chances of getting away with anything in PG57, more and more escape from Spittal was looking like a possibility — with the right plan.

Thanks to the resourcefulness of some of the prisoners, we also had quite another kind of diversion, a precious one that brought us word from the outside world: a wireless. I don't know where they got the parts from, but they kept them stored in half a dozen different places all around the camp, always changing their locations. We would come together at about 4 p.m. each day, in a different room each time, bringing with us all the parts. We'd post some 'cockatoos' — lookouts — in the hallway of the building we were in. If the Germans came along, they'd make a bit of noise, and we'd know to dismantle the radio and hide the parts. We were never caught. Maybe the guards knew what we were up to but could never catch us at it.

We would listen to the BBC from London, in English, clear as day. So we knew exactly what was going on in the war now, how the Allies were faring on the Russian front, how the Pacific war was going. We knew that things were turning our way. We probably knew more than our captors. It helped to keep us in reasonably good spirits, to look after ourselves, to have a shave every day — there was a world out there that we were part of. It also fed my ideas of escape. I had a dream around about that time that I did escape. It was a vivid dream, of me running through a forest of pine trees. When I woke I didn't want to dream about it any more, but to come up with a proper plan and do it.

Meanwhile, we found many other ways to amuse ourselves. One day, we organised an entire race meeting. We dreamed up imaginary horses, put them into imaginary fields and had pretend bookies lay the pretend odds. We drew up a very smart-looking program for the Spittal Turf Club, listing all the races and officials. Very elaborate it was. Of course, there were no real races, no real bets, but it diverted us thoroughly for a whole day.

One of our favourite pastimes was taunting the guards, just with that bit of broken English-German banter over who was going to win the war, but with our BBC listening, after we'd heard the news that Berlin had taken a heavy air raid in November, we got a bit cheekier. 'Bomber Berlin, Bomber Berlin,' we would chant at them. A bit stupid when you think about it, as they must have wondered how on earth we knew. And it rebounded on us tragically one day. One guard became

A bloke in drag off to the races with his mates at Stalag 18 A/Z.
I don't know who these guys are, but the 'amusements' were the same all over the camps.

quite agitated as some of our boys teased him — the war no doubt was wearing him down, getting to him, too, as it was clear that Germany was in trouble. He slammed the bolt into his rifle, as if to say, 'Shut up or I'll shoot you,' but as he did the magazine fell out, scattering bullets all over the ground. Our boys laughed uproariously at this, which infuriated him even more. He was screaming at them now. Quickly, an officer came out, took one look at the situation, and ordered all of us to return to our huts. 'Inside, everyone!' he commanded. 'Now!' We did as we were told.

Just inside the gate was a new compound containing some American prisoners. I think they were air force. They hadn't heard what was going on outside, nor the officer's order for everyone to remain indoors. One of them picked up a dish of water and walked outside to empty it and a guard shot him dead. Bang, just like that. The order had been that nobody was to go outside. So he shot an unarmed prisoner. We laid off the taunts for a while after that.

~

All in all, I did it pretty easy in Stalag 18 A/Z. I looked after myself as best I could and used up plenty of time picking the lice out of my clothes and hair. Conditions were not very hygienic, of course, and our great friends the body lice were everywhere — not as bad as at PG57, but nearly. There were all those other bugs of disease, too, because of the lice and the conditions and the cold. I must have become immune to them, I suppose, because my health, fortunately, remained pretty good.

I'd think about the blokes who had died in PG57, and not necessarily of infections or being shot, but because of malnutrition, from that damned rice and caterpillar soup. Years later, I'd come to understand that if you eat polished rice continually and pretty much exclusively, you retain liquid. Brown rice, with the husk on, is good for you. But polished rice, without greens or something to supplement it, is not — there's no thiamine in it. Liquids build up in the system, somehow causing swelling in the chest and putting pressure on the heart. It's called beriberi. Blokes would have heart attacks from it. A bloke would wake up in the morning and find his mate dead beside him. I didn't know what caused it at the time, but it happened to about a dozen blokes in Italy. It wasn't going to happen to me here in Spittal. We were still hungry all the time, but that potato soup was so much more nutritious than the soup at PG57 — I knew that, I could feel it — and the Germans were much better at getting our Red Cross rations to us. Yet sickness started to play on my mind as winter set in, like a mouldy old potato.

I didn't want to get sick and I didn't want to die in a POW camp. Nor did I want to stay there for the rest of the war. I didn't know how long the fighting was going to continue. A lot of blokes were resigned to being prisoners for the duration of the war, with no intention of escaping. I never was, not really, except for those first couple of months in Italy, when it seemed impossible to even think about escape. For a start, I felt ashamed to be a POW. My attitude was that if I was locked away behind barbed wire, it meant I hadn't done my job. I'd surrendered to the enemy and I should not have. I should have stayed on the battlefield and fought until I died. Dead hero or live coward? I thought about it all the time; and the more I languished, the more I thought about it. I couldn't get away from the idea that it wasn't right that I was in a prison camp while others were still fighting and dying in their thousands.

Eric Batty, my roommate, felt the same way. He'd been taken prisoner in Greece in '41, and transported by train through the Balkans to Austria. Eric hated being in the camp, and he especially hated the Germans. He'd 'escaped' several times already. He got out once through a tunnel, another time by climbing the electrified perimeter fence of a camp during a power failure, a third time by crawling through a drain. But he wasn't really serious about escaping then. How could he have been? He was alone, with no resources and no chance. It was more, as it always was with him in the camp, a way of getting up the Germans' noses, of saying, 'Bugger them.' He called these forays for freedom the Spring Handicap, as just about all he'd achieve each time was to sneak out and pick a few blackberries before being caught. And each time he'd been caught he'd done time in the German military prison — twenty-eight days apiece — where they'd beat him up to beat the impulse out of him. I think that's why he hated the Germans so much.

It was winter now, though, and our talk of escape was just that for the time being: a talkfest. But Eric was clear in his intentions as we talked. 'Wait until this spring comes,' he would say, 'and then I'm off again for good. I'm going to clear out.'

The notion of a serious escape came to me slowly. It was not as if I was looking through the wire every day and saying, 'I'm going.' But Eric set my mind to work. So did another bloke, Allan Berry, a West Australian, with whom I'd formed a good friendship. His real name was Arnold but everyone called him Allan, even his family, and he was a lad pretty much like me, a knockabout country boy, a couple of years older, like Eric, but who'd never settled at any particular job. Like plenty of us he'd started out working during the Depression and had gone from job to job. He was also in my battalion in Africa, but in another company, and I hadn't known him well then. The last time I'd seen him before meeting up with him again in Spittal was a brief glimpse of him in the prison camp at Benghazi, and he'd been in an awful way. He'd been taken prisoner at El Alamein in July and had done it hard at the Benghazi camp. There had been no cover, just a few tents, where some could sleep, others had to sleep in the sand. It was primitive. Allan told me he went to a doctor there and said, 'I haven't been to the toilet for a week.' The doctor said: 'Well, what do you think you're going to shit? You're not getting anything to eat.' He said he used to have to pick the dried shit out of his backside with his fingers. When I first saw him at Spittal, with some flesh back on him, I didn't recognise him. At Benghazi, he had been just skin and bone. He had looked the same from in front or behind: ribs sticking out everywhere. Allan had been a good footballer earlier in the war, the star of the battalion team, but Benghazi had turned him into a mess — those Italians really were mongrels.

Now that he was over the worst of that ordeal, he was also drawn to the idea of escape. Another Kiwi by the name of Matthew Gibson was in on the idea, too. Just thinking about it kept us going.

It was still only early January, a long time till spring. Eric, Allan, Matthew and I knew our best chance of escaping in the spring was to get to a work camp, which would give us an opportunity to be out and about, with minimum supervision, on farms and in quarries, and allow us to recondition our bodies for the physical challenges we would face on the run. The problem was that all four of us were NCOs. Eric was a corporal, the rest sergeants. And the Germans had a thing about NCOs: they wouldn't let them go out to work. They figured that NCOs were too intelligent and might find ways to shoot through. They were right at least about the latter. We hatched a plan.

Privates, who were compelled to go out and work, used all sorts of tricks to get out of it. Many, of course, didn't object to the opportunity to break the monotony of camp life, but plenty of others resented the idea of being forced to effectively work for the German war effort. One trick to avoid it was to tap your knee repeatedly with a wet, knotted towel, which would cause fluid to rise on the knee and make you hobble. I didn't like the idea of those guys deliberately harming themselves like that in a prison camp, where medical care was minimal — if you did hurt yourself badly, you'd have to live with it — but they did it anyway. Another trick was to pretend to be an NCO. Some prisoners would put stripes on their shoulders; they would write to Australia House in London to let them know they'd arranged 'promotions' for themselves, and though they wouldn't be paid as NCOs, Australia House would approve these recommendations, on the principle that every POW who didn't work was one less man the enemy could use for its own benefit. They were called 'barbed-wire NCOs'.

We decided to use reverse psychology. The next time the guards ordered all privates to line up for work, we hid our paybooks, which identified us as NCOs, and lined up, too. When the doctor declared us fit to work, we pretended to protest. 'I don't have to work,' I said, 'I'm a sergeant.'

'Where's your proof?' he asked. 'Where's your paybook?' When I said I couldn't find it, he said, 'If you don't have your paybook, out to work you go.' He wasn't having any of this business of prisoners bunging on stripes and not working. Which, of course, was just the reaction we wanted from him.

Looked like we were on our way — out of this stalag, at least.

11

TAKING OUR CHANCES

It was late January, 1944, still winter, but coming out of the depths, when we were sent from Spittal by train to Graz, about seventy or eighty miles east, not far from the Hungarian border. It was quite a large town, a small city, really, and pretty with its old buildings — all red roofs and spires — and the prison camp there was not too far from the centre of the place. When we arrived, we weren't interested in sightseeing: straight off we asked what sort of work the prisoners did, disappointed we'd found ourselves in a town, rather than in the countryside. We were told that work parties were currently digging an air raid shelter in a rock escarpment near town. We said we'd be buggered if we were going to dig an air raid shelter for the Germans. That was not the sort of work prisoners were supposed to be assigned — we weren't supposed to be involved in building or making anything for war use, and we didn't want to be building something for the Germans' protection. We refused to go out to work.

So the guards brought in their superior, a Major Benedict, to try to force us. He was livid at our attitude. He said he was going to have us all shot if we didn't go to work. But Matthew could speak fluent German — he was one of those blokes who was just exceptionally clever that way, picking up German from his captors — he was a big bloke, too — and he gave the major as good as he got. He was amazing. He said he would contact the Red Cross and invoke the Geneva Convention, report this Major Benedict for threatening to shoot unarmed prisoners. Then we all produced our paybooks to emphasise the point: don't mess with the superior intelligence of NCOs. It'd be better to be sent back to Spittal than put up with this. We told him we wanted to work, but not against the rules. Finally, the major relented and, rather than sending us back, asked us what sort of work we wanted to do. We told him, disingenuously, that we were all farmers from Australia and New Zealand. We weren't used to being in cities or working in factories or mines; we were just hicks and wanted to work on the land. Maybe it was that or it was our appeal about the 'rules' that got to him, who knows, but he said he'd find something for us.

While we were waiting for our assignment in that prison camp at Graz, we would see waves of Boston bombers fly over every day to attack German bases, factories and railway lines. They came from North Africa, mostly Tunisia, from the many aerodromes the Allies used as bases for their air force. The Germans were long gone from Africa. The Allies had used an elaborate decoy to lure them to southern Italy. And now North Africa was secure, with one Allied army having come from the west, from Morocco, and the other from Egypt in the east, making the airstrips well protected and safe — ideal launch pads for bombing raids into Europe.

The bombers would fly low over us, barely five hundred feet above our heads. You could just about see the rivets in the wings and the pilots in their cockpits. I wondered at the time why they flew at such low altitude; we'd only ever seen bombers doing their job two or three thousand feet up. I'd realise later that the reason they were coming in at such a low angle was that they gave the Germans only one shot at them with their 'ack ack' — anti-aircraft — guns, and made it tricky for the Germans, with the low trajectory, to avoid shelling their own town and civilians. These bombers would swoop in from over the surrounding mountains, drop their bombs in perfect sequence as if along an invisible line, and then were gone.

Some days, they bombed their way right past our camp. You'd see the bombs falling from the planes. Lots of prisoners

Air Force Historical Research Agency

One of our Allied Boston bombers — the sight of them over Graz gave us heart.

ran inside when they saw this. But I didn't like that idea. I thought that the timber buildings offered no protection from a bomb, anyway, and inside them you ran the risk of being killed by the splintered wood or burned to death. I would lie on my back on the ground and watch the bombs fall. Because of the low altitude of the planes, and the trajectory of the bombs as they fell, you thought every second one was going to hit you, even though they were really about two hundred yards away. It was a pretty scary sight.

But the bombers must have known where the prison camp was, and they were so skilful and accurate that no bomb came close to us. They zeroed in on the oil refinery at Graz, dropping bombs all the way. In an odd way, this was encouragement for the four of us. The war was turning, the Allies were coming, the

Germans were under siege. It emboldened us even more in our escape plans.

And it emboldened me in particular. We'd only been there a week or so when, quite spontaneously, I decided I'd have a little outing on my own — just for fun, and to test the laxness of the guards at this camp, I suppose. Each day, six men were assigned to go down to the post office in the town to pick up mail and parcels for the POWs, and this day, as I was watching those chosen for post office detail start to file out, I said to the bloke standing next to me, 'How about we go, too?' I can't remember his name, sadly; I'd only known him for five minutes, but he fell in with me behind the six, and off we went, two by two. The guards' laxness was in full evidence: no-one stopped us. Eight must have not have seemed so different a number from six to their careless glance. I wasn't even thinking about the possible consequences; I just wanted to do it. And I had no intention of not returning.

Geez, it felt good, just to be out and about, in the town, looking at the shops, not that there was much in them. While we were there I fell into conversation with a pleasant Austrian woman in the street. She had holidayed in England in 1938 and could speak good English. 'How are you going?' she asked. 'How are they treating you in there?' She wasn't afraid, and she certainly wasn't contemptuous. I think educated people well understood what was going on in the war; they were not in the least brainwashed by the propaganda. I don't think she could have known, though, how pleasant it was for me just to have a short chat with a person in the street, as if I was one, too.

But the smile would be wiped from my face when we got back to the camp and one of the boys yelled at me through the fence, 'You're gone. You're gone.' There had been a roll call while we were away, and it had become clear that two prisoners were missing. The Germans didn't know who; just that they were two short in their count.

Oh shit, I thought. They're going to get us. What am I going to say to them: 'Oh, well, really, I had no intention of escaping today. I just wanted to have a gander in town because I felt like it'? The consequences only hit home then: twenty-eight days in the military prison, being belted for intention to escape, but really just for being a smart arse. We were stopped ten feet short of the gate, and the guard there was taking names and numbers. When my turn came, I don't know where I got the arse from, but I simply walked up to the guard and said, 'Yeah, she's right.' Then I kept walking into the camp. Somehow it worked. But they got the whole camp out again for another roll call because they knew that something was wrong. They just could not figure out what. A couple of sayings I'd read in books had stuck in my head, perhaps: 'Boldness, be my friend', and 'It's not how brave you are, it's what you do at that moment'. I was pretty cool; I'd got away with it but I was very well aware of the close shave.

It didn't stop me from having another outing, this time with Allan and Eric. It was early February now, no snow on the ground, but again, no intention of escaping. We wouldn't have survived out there, too cold and no food in the fields to forage, and as yet we still had no firm plan. It was just something to do, to see if we could get under the wire, sneak out, have a look around, and sneak back, in the dark. Slack as the guards might have been, the camp was well secured at night, with searchlights on two towers which sat diagonally opposite on the corners of the compound square, with attendant sentries and machine guns. The perimeter of the square consisted of two wire fences, inner and outer — both about ten feet high — forming a laneway about six or eight feet wide. At the bottom of the inner fence, about six inches above the ground, lay the lowest of the barbed-wire threads. Over four or five days, every time we took a walk around the compound, we would put our boots under that bottom wire at the same point and give it a heave, till we found that it had slackened enough for us to be able to lift it up eighteen or so inches, more than enough to get under. So, having achieved that, we waited for dark and decided to have a night out. When I think about it now, it was bloody stupid; it could easily have ruined any plan for escape there and then. If caught, at the least we'd have been punished and separated, and at the worst shot dead on the spot. But we did it anyway.

Eric went first. He had crawled under the inner wire and was in the laneway between the two fences when the searchlight fell directly on him. Those lights swept down each of their lanes every two or three minutes as a matter of routine, so it wasn't a surprise; we didn't think the sentries above would be looking for anything in particular.

'Lie along the wire, lie along the wire,' we hissed at Eric, and he did: flattened himself facedown on the ground parallel to the wire, and it worked. His dark shape would have looked no different from the shadows of the fence poles amid the many shadows along the laneway. No-one saw him. He waited until it was dark again, then went on, scurrying under the outer wire, which was high enough to get under easily. So Allan and myself did the same: crawled under the inner wire into the laneway, lay there while the searchlight swept over us, then when it was dark again crawled under the outside wire. It was a kind of practice escape, mental preparation for the real thing.

We went under the wire three nights in a row, gradually becoming more and more bold. On that first night, only a few hundred yards from the wire, we stumbled across what looked like an empty army mess — it was a large open-ended hall that might have serviced troops passing through with meals and digs. In it, we found food, three-legged stools and coils of flex wire. We broke up a couple of the stools and took them back to the camp to use in the heater. We also took a frying pan. Then we got ourselves back into the camp the same way we left, under the wire, timing our movements to avoid the searchlight — effectively breaking into the camp again.

On the third night, we thought we would venture further out and have a look around Graz. We were walking down the road when suddenly we heard voices coming towards us in the dark. We dived down an embankment beside the road and waited, hardly daring to breathe, until they had passed. But it brought us to our senses. We'd proved the point to ourselves: we could do it, we had the nerve, and there was no reason to push our luck further.

Not long afterwards we received our work assignment. We were sent to a prison farm camp area, called Arbeitskommando 410L. Just the four of us, too. It was incredibly lucky we were allowed to stay together, that's for sure. We were put to work on a group of small farms in a tiny village called Petzendorf, about twenty miles south of Graz, back towards the Slovenian border again — not that we had any clear idea of where we were yet. There was another, bigger farm camp at Dobl, a couple of miles away. We weren't housed in a camp, though, but in Petzendorf itself. Our digs looked to be what might have been an old lockup attached to one of the houses, and we shared the cells with eight others, all Brits. There were only five or six houses in the whole place, on one side of a track, and the farmland, only seven or eight acres apiece, on the other side. It was very cosy. Phase one of our plan had been achieved.

While we were there, I wore a type of beret — just a plain standard-issue military thing with no markings on it — and I took to sticking a white turkey feather in the band of it. The locals, who were all quite nice people, didn't know what to make of it. 'Why do you wear the white feather?' they would ask in broken English when they passed me on the track. 'No good! Coward!' As an added irony, in German, the pronunciation of my name Brough — 'bruff' — sounds a little like *brav*, their word for brave, and they would say, 'You are brave soldier — or coward?' I would just laugh at them. I enjoyed the idea that it stirred them up a bit. Even though they were pleasant, in my mind, they were on the wrong side in the war. Looking back, I must have been a pretty cocky young bloke then, or maybe it was that I could feel freedom getting closer. Some were cockier still — I knew of at least one bloke from another farm camp who took some mutually satisfying liberties with a lonesome local housewife, risking twenty-eight days of military prison beatings for each stolen kiss.

None of that type of playing up for the likes of me. I was too busy cleaning out cow stalls and helping to sow oats, which was no big deal for a country lad. I was working with a boy of about twelve one day, one of the farmers' kids, and we were sent to repair a wire fence. He had some staples and a hammer, and I had to hold the wire while he hammered the staples into the fence post. Just as he went to hit the staple, I would drop the wire, causing him to miss. I did it four or five times. A pretty mean-minded prank, I guess, to pick on a kid, but again I enjoyed anything that felt like I was impeding the German war effort and making things hard for them. It drove the boy so mad, though, he reported me to the guard. 'Behave yourself,' the guard warned me, 'or you'll go back inside,' meaning back inside the lockup we were sent to when not working.

I behaved myself. The four of us did, ever mindful of this opportunity to get ourselves fit and strong. We knew our fitness would be a key to survival once we escaped. On Sundays, we'd have a day off — the whole village did, in accordance with their devout Catholicism — and we would walk the few miles to the Dobl camp and back again to get some strength and condition in our legs. We were unguarded and easily identifiable as prisoners. One day at Dobl, Allan made a great find for us: he was able to swap his British-issue overcoat for a much more essential item — a compass owned by a Polish prisoner there.

At that time, before we had a proper sense of exactly where we were, we thought we might make our escape across Hungary then through Romania. It would have entailed crossing the Danube River — a thought that was nothing short of terrifying for someone with my swimming ability, but I was so fired up to be off by now, I'd have done it for sure. Fortunately, that plan was quickly scrapped when, at Dobl again, we met up with some British POWs who had a map of

Austria, which would set our course. We would head south, into Slovenia. We asked to borrow the map and set about trying to make ourselves a copy by tracing it onto the greaseproof paper that lined our Red Cross biscuit tins. We tried for a week but to no avail. That type of paper is impossible to draw on without a decent pen. We needed all the detail: the roads, the borders, the heights of the mountains, and we couldn't come up with a legible tracing.

In the end we decided to pinch the map. We reported back to the British POWs that our quarters had been raided and searched, and the map confiscated. We did the dirty on them, really. We justified it by reasoning that they had had the map for a few years and done nothing with it. It was our turn now.

It still might so easily have all gone wrong. Only three or four days before we intended to escape, Eric pinched the best vest of one of the farmers, planning to use it as a disguise on our travels. It was a conspicuous vest, the one the farmer wore to church on Sundays. Eric hid it in our cell, under the wood by the heater, but after a complaint from the farmer, the guards searched the room and found it. They were very suspicious, telling us they were thinking of sending a permanent guard to keep watch over us. But they found nothing else. Fortunately Allan had our compass and map safely tucked away on his person. But the close call made us doubly determined to make our break soon — we couldn't have done it with a permanent guard hanging about. Easter was coming, with its full moon, and we set our date.

In a peculiar way, we had built up a rapport with the farmers, especially the one who housed us in those cells on his property. While we were there, Eric had developed the habit of getting into the chook pen and sucking the yolks out of the eggs, carelessly leaving the hollow egg shells behind, and now, on Good Friday morning, with only the daylight hours to count till we'd make our escape, the farmer invited us all in for breakfast — and Easter eggs, the painted variety, decorated by the family for their Sunday celebrations, as was the local custom. I didn't go, but Eric went along, and when he sat down at the farmer's table, with all the family there, he was presented with a painted egg — with two holes in it. The farmer and his family laughed heartily. They knew what he had been up to, but didn't mind. This was their joke in reply. They, as farm people, and we, as prisoners, were ordinary folk with plenty in common, just caught up on opposite sides in the ugliness of war. They showed us kindnesses that I didn't appreciate much at the time. For morning tea they'd give us strips of cured bacon called *Speck*, which was pretty revolting but meant to give us a bit of fat, necessary in the European winter. These people didn't have much — no money, nothing but what they produced on the land, and what they produced they shared. An old-world way of living, it was.

As for me, I'd been too keyed up for sentimentality or Easter celebrations of any sort. Our plans were made, and the day before we'd gathered all the food we thought we'd need. All the prisoners' tucker, including the stores of Red Cross parcels, was kept locked up in a cellar under another of the houses. Prisoners were supposed to go down in pairs once a week for supplies, but the evening before our breakout, all twelve of us went together for the key. Laxity was our friend again and we were all let into the store. We stuffed our trousers and socks with supplies: dried fruit, cocoa, powdered milk, cheese, biscuits and as many tins as we could manage. Later, we swapped what we could with the other blokes, perishables for non-perishables mostly. We couldn't take any

Red Cross parcel day for three prisoner-workers. Those parcels were key to our plans.

tins of meat with us. One of the girls on the farm would puncture any tins of meat and other non-perishables that might go stale or rancid when opened, as per her instructions, to make sure that no-one could stow them away. We knew we could only take on our escape whatever we could carry on our bodies and in haversacks — we filled four haversacks, enough food for several weeks. We hid our stash away overnight as best we could under the wood by the heater. Then we were ready.

Although they helped us gather that food, the eight Brits we'd been living with had been apprehensive about our escape plans all along, and now the night had come they were only more so. 'What will happen to us when they find out you're gone?' they asked. Their anxiety was understandable. They'd be interrogated, at the least, as to where we'd gone and how we'd escaped. Then, at the last minute, Matthew, the other Kiwi among us, pulled out, too. He said he had a bad knee, but I think it might have more likely been a faint heart; and I don't blame him. The risks we were about to take were massive. But it was a bad break for us in one way: Matthew's fluent German was a skill that would have come in handy. Nevertheless, the rest of us — Eric, Allan and me — were determined to go ahead.

~

We made our break, just as we planned, on the night of April 8, 1944 — that same Good Friday. What we did not know at the time was that there had been a mass escape from a high-security camp called Stalag Luft III — the one made famous in the film *The Great Escape*. The Germans were ropable, and had given orders that when the escapees were rounded up, two-thirds should be executed. I think fifty or sixty died this way: shot through the head in cold blood. It also meant that the Germans were on extra alert for escapees from other prison camps. The village of Petzendorf and its surrounds would have been crawling with guards. But we didn't know anything about it, which probably was just as well.

The big moment for us came. It was a quarter to nine. We knew that the guard who locked us up at night in the cells didn't live on the premises and didn't stay overnight. One of the Brits had found a way to work the lock from the inside, using a piece of wire, and he opened the door for us — and left it open. At least, I hope he did, or else it would have been obvious to the Germans how the door had been opened. As it was, the Brits were fretful, wondering what would become of them when the Germans discovered we had gone. But with the adrenalin and anticipation cranking up in the three of us, it was hard to feel too sympathetic for those who were staying behind. They had had their chance and declined. We were taking ours.

Frustrated at POWs escaping all the time, the Germans had set up high-security prisons. This is the famous Colditz castle.

12
ON THE RUN

We set out wearing standard-issue British battledress uniform, as supplied by the Red Cross, good sturdy woollen cloth, with jackets that fitted at the waist to keep the cold out, but we had no overcoats; they would have been too heavy to carry, especially if wet, and would have slowed us down. We didn't have groundsheets, waterproofing or blankets. Basically, we had what we were wearing, what was in our pockets and what was in the four small haversacks we carried between us. We padded down the corridor with our boots off, so as to make no noise on the stone floor. On the outside steps we sat down to put our boots back on and looked at one another, each taking a silent, deep breath. We had escaped our cells — but we had always known that would be the easy part.

Most escapees made no firm plans at all, but wandered about with the vague idea of getting on a train somewhere. Mostly they didn't get far. We had a plan, step-by-step, and the first step was that we would walk as far as we could on that night, at least fifteen miles. We figured that would put us beyond the range of a likely search when we were discovered missing the next dawn. We would travel at night — the darkness would be our friend — and lay up where we could during the day.

The night was cold, but clear and bright. It was Easter, remember, full moon. We had our compass to guide us and set off due south, in the direction of the Drau River. Vaguely in the back of our minds, the larger plan was to keep heading south, through Slovenia and then down to the Adriatic Sea, where we would try to get our hands on a boat to row to Italy. But that would be days and weeks away, if we made it at all. We had to keep to the small steps, one at a time.

We went for our lives. This was rural Central Europe — woodlands, lots of small farm plots, but no fences, dotted with little villages just like Petzendorf — and we made ground quickly. Adrenalin and nerves kept us going at a cracking pace. Finally, at around 3.30 a.m., after probably making fifteen or twenty miles, we sensed a bit of the paleness in the sky that meant dawn was coming and we would have to look for somewhere to hide out. We took refuge in a copse of young pine trees, around ten or fifteen feet high, which lay inside what looked to be a little informal parkland, full of shrubs and trees. Because we had been through a couple of depressions filled with water during the night, our boots and socks were wet, so we took them off and hung the socks in the trees to dry. Then we nestled down in among the pines, trying to make ourselves as invisible as we could.

Around midday or early in the afternoon we heard voices. There was a track through the woods, and coming down it was a large party of women and children. It was Easter Saturday, a holiday, and they were in a jovial mood. They were heading towards a cluster of houses on a hill about 400 yards away. We hadn't noticed them in the night. The kids were playing a type of cowboys and Indians, ducking in and out of the trees. Three of them, aged around six or seven, stumbled into our little thicket and saw our socks hung up on the branches. '*Shau! Shau!*' they began to shout. Look! Look! We held our breath as we stared at them and they stared straight at us. They took off towards the rest of the group, trying to draw their mothers' attention to us.

We thought we'd better move, and quickly, in case any of the adults came to investigate. We put our socks and boots back on and headed for the track, walking in the direction from which the party had come, figuring that their scents might help to disguise ours if they sent dogs out after us. But after only about a hundred yards or so, we spotted a big pile of leaves about two feet thick — mulched-up old oak leaves,

I think they were, in a heap big enough for three. They must have been sitting there since winter, waiting for us to come along. With scarcely a moment's hesitation, we decided to bury ourselves in them and wait until dark. Fortunately the kids' excited story of the strangers in the trees must have held little interest for their mothers and no-one came.

That was probably the worst day of all, that first day. Even in early spring, it would be at least 7.30 p.m. before it was dark enough for us to get up and move on. The ground was cold and damp, and we nearly froze to death waiting for night to fall so we could set out again. The worst hours were from about 4 or 5 p.m. with that damp cold sinking into you with the coming dusk, making you ache to the core. It was an experience we'd come to know all too well. We had no blankets, as I've said, nor anything to sleep on. We learned to kip on the hard ground, back-to-belly, cuddling one another for warmth and rotating every half-hour or so — the best place to be was in the middle. And while we slept, the sweat in our clothes and on our skins would cool and freeze as the sun began to set. When we woke, our clothes would be stiff and it would be ten minutes before we could say a word to each other, we were so cold. But we had no choice other than to get moving again. We didn't feel sorry for ourselves; we couldn't afford that. We just had to get up and go.

~

The second night, Easter Saturday night, we made our way along a gully, about fifty yards down behind the houses on the hill, which were all lit up, full of people enjoying their holiday, and no doubt including the same women and children we'd seen during the day. Suddenly, a little fox terrier emerged from one of the houses and began to follow us, yapping all the way. We were petrified that its barking would raise the alarm. We muttered at it to go away. Eventually, thankfully, it did. It was another of the many lucky breaks we would have on our expedition.

A little further along the way, we came across a typical village. Just like Petzendorf, it consisted of a line of simple houses along one side of a track, with a few acres of farmland across from each, now fallow and bare and black. There was also a small common amid the farms. In the summer, the villagers would turn their cattle out onto the common, but this was early spring, and most of the livestock was still indoors. We picked our way in the darkness around the outskirts of the village farmland and across one fence. Amazingly, it was the only such fence we would encounter throughout our flight. So unlike the rural countryside of my homeland, in Victoria, and Australia generally, with its much larger acreages and miles of fences, this country was literally open rolling pastures, not even hedges to jump, and again we made good ground that night.

As the second night gave way to the first light of dawn, we decided to take a risk — well, we had no choice but to, as

Fotosearch 71056762

A typical Austrian village with its church steeple and farmhouses — we did our best to avoid them, but this part of Europe is so well populated it wasn't always easy.

the light was gathering and we needed somewhere to hide for the day. Ahead lay another village, and we walked straight into it. It was still early and no-one was about, thankfully. But where to hide? There were houses on one side of the track and a big wooden building on the other, which turned out to be a barn. We scuttled to the back of this barn, found a ladder and climbed up to a loft that was full of hay. So we made ourselves as comfortable as we could and settled in for the day. Compared with our previous day's accommodation this was five-star.

A while later, we heard the clamour of voices. Cautiously, we looked out through cracks in the boards of the barn wall and saw that the track was full of people dressed in their finest. It was Easter Sunday morning and they were off to church. We felt we were in a dicey position, right among those villagers. They were mostly women and children, and a few old men, as the majority of men of working age would've been off at war. We didn't know what these people would make of us if they found us — but we were absolutely certain that it would be the end of our escape. If any of them had had reason to check the barn that day, we would have been cornered, and no doubt trapped till the local Gestapo or guard arrived to interrogate us, belt us, and send us off for twenty-eight days in the military prison. They'd want to know where we got our compass, our map of Austria, our food, and possibly try to beat it out of us. But we were lucky again: saved by people too busy enjoying their holidays.

Later that morning, Eric spotted a Frenchman leaning against the barn and woke us. The man was smoking a cigarette, and we knew he was French by the beret and bits and pieces of the uniform he was wearing. Almost certainly he would have been a POW of sorts, on parole from forced labour on a farm. There were many like him across Austria and Germany. They were free to move around when they were not working, but not to go home to France. If any one of them broke their parole, the Germans would send word to France and have his farm burned down. These French prisoners had nowhere to go. They couldn't go home, they couldn't leave Europe, they had no choice but to work and hope. It must have been a wretched life.

Eric put his mouth to the door of the barn and called to the Frenchman in a loud whisper, in a mock French accent: 'François? François?' He acknowledged that he had heard, so Eric climbed down and had a chat to him in the cover of the doorway — by chat I mean a fair bit of sign language and the only French word Eric could think of for food, which was 'biscuit', or 'bis-coo-eet', as Eric was pronouncing it. The Frenchman appeared to promise he would come back after dark with some biscuits for us. He was as good as his word, perhaps glad that someone was escaping even if he couldn't, and soon after sunset, he came back with a sack of biscuits — a great supplement to our own supplies, every little bit helped. We thanked him profusely, then cleared off. This wasn't the time to stop to socialise or count our blessings.

The lights were on in all the houses as we made our way to a vacant lot between them, directly across from the barn. Beyond the lot was a hill that rose up behind the village. We hadn't gone far up that hill when we found ourselves in a wilderness of blackberries. There was no fruit on them — too early in the spring for that — and there was nothing for it but to clamber through their thorny canes, scratching our hands and faces and cursing. We couldn't see how far this blackberry patch stretched, but we had to keep going — no alternative — so we did.

After what seemed like endless hours, when we finally broke free of the blackberry bushes, we stopped for a spell to catch our breath and inspect our scratches. Distantly, we could hear a saxophone playing somewhere, a beautifully melodic sound carrying through the cold night air. I thought it was the loveliest thing I had heard in years. It was a reminder of civilisation, which now seemed to us far away and long ago. It suddenly made me realise what this war had taken from me, and all that had changed in me, and it left me feeling homesick and melancholy. It was just the idea, I suppose, that someone was free to sit there and play a tune. How long would it be before I could sit around with my mates and listen to a band playing or have a dance?

But that moment of sentimentality was short-lived. We couldn't rest for long, couldn't lose too much time; we had to plough on down the other side of the hill and back into farmland. Later that night, we found ourselves in a field full of some kind of crop. We couldn't see what it was or its colour in the dark, but I picked a leaf or two and popped it into my mouth. I could immediately taste the green freshness of rapeseed. It is a brassica plant, like cauliflower, the crop we take canola oil from these days. It tasted a bit like cabbage and is often used to feed cattle. Well, for us it was a feast of green vegetable. How long had it been since we'd had greens! We had a thorough feed, stuffed ourselves, our bodies craving those vitamins, then we filled up a dixie — one of our all-purpose eating and drinking vessels — with supplies and stuffed our pockets, too. The farmer who worked that field must have wondered what strange, hungry animals had raided his crop when he saw the damage the next day.

But the night was still on us and we kept going, ploughing on, fighting tiredness, stopping periodically to rest, crouching on the ground. We were making good pace again, and as we went along in silence I felt another change come over me, over us: it seemed to me that we were becoming part of the landscape, our senses, our instincts constantly alert to our survival, like animals. In our own way, we were turning wild.

~

As dawn began to break on the third day of our great escape, we found ourselves in open, green, sloping grasslands, about thirty acres nestled in a small valley, and once again we had to look around for somewhere to hide. We soon discovered an old watercourse snaking down the hill. It looked to be a stormwater channel whose sides had been washed away by heavy rain, creating concave banks. We climbed down into the drain and tucked ourselves away under the curved ledge of the banks, each in a different place. We lay there all day, not moving, not saying a word to each other, simply keeping our positions, sleeping in snatches. We knew that we were vulnerable out there in the open, and any loose word or stray movement might have meant capture or death; who knew? It made for a long, silent, uncomfortable day: you don't get a much colder and damper and danker spot than a shady drain — I suppose at least we should have been grateful the stream wasn't flowing at the time.

Late afternoon was the worst, as usual. Just about every joint in my body had seized up and I was longing to move. Then I heard voices, and suddenly, I looked up to see the legs of a kid, a boy of about eight or nine leaping over the drain, right above my head. Then another boy. I don't know, perhaps there were three or four of them, all chatting away and laughing. Just playing about, being young boys. I could just about have reached out and tripped them if I had wanted. Luckily, they did not see me or Eric or Allan, and moved on somewhere else to play.

At dusk, without saying a word, but by some form of mute understanding, we regrouped where we'd noticed this creek in the morning, just before we'd hidden ourselves. Now we decided we'd have a wash in it and fill our water bottles. We'd only been gone a couple of days, and already we were beginning to stink. Actually, before we'd even left the camp we'd decided that we were going to make an effort to have a proper wash when we could and shave at least once every couple of days, if not every day, keep our hair combed, and look as tidy as we could. The reason was that, apart from

The type of beautiful, idyllic pastureland we crossed on our journey.
Back then, though, it was full of danger for us, at every turn.

trying to keep the lice populations on our bodies to a minimum, we figured that it would help our morale to stay strong if we made these small gestures towards self-respect. If you look like a hobo, you'll more than likely feel like one; but we were soldiers. We wouldn't get away with growing straggly beards in the army so why should we here? We'd brought soap with us and a razor, which we all shared and which we sharpened on a piece of broken bottle. That razor would last us throughout our adventures. But for now, having a wash in that fresh water was our objective.

A few yards off, there was a little bridge across the creek, just wide enough for a horse and cart, and we were near completing our ablutions when an Austrian man came along leading his horse, spotted us, and asked what we were doing. We couldn't do anything but keep our nerve. With our poker faces we tried to tell him in our makeshift German that we were German troops on leave having a bit of a look around. Our German for a start was appalling — we had about two dozen words between us, and the rest made up with bad but valiant attempts at a German accent. The Austrian bloke nodded, seeming friendly enough. 'Good, good,' he responded. He was going on to his village, he said, but would come back later if we liked and pick us up. We would have a good night: drinking, dancing, sleeping comfortably. We told him that was very kind of him. But we were sure he didn't believe us; who would? To add to our 'German' we were wearing British uniforms: we couldn't know if he had any idea of what a British uniform looked like, but we were very obviously three soldiers and not from a German army — even if we sounded like we should have been in a vaudeville show. As soon as he was gone, so were we, off on another long night's walk, due south.

The weather had remained miraculously kind to us. But on this night, the sky became overcast, making the it darker and navigation more difficult. We had no torch, only Allan's cigarette lighter, to read the compass by — and for Allan to have a smoke — and we used it sparingly, to conserve the fuel in it and so as not to draw attention to ourselves. If you were to make a scene in a movie of this part of an escaped POW's journey, it'd just be a black screen with occasional glimpses of silver moonlight reflecting off the cloud. Most importantly for us, though, the rain had stayed away, which was a blessing during both the long night walks up hill and down dale, and the long unmoving days.

As dawn broke the next day we came to a forest of young pine trees. We settled into a dense little copse, but at about ten o'clock, we heard the sound of axes. Men were working in the forest, less than a hundred yards away. We could hear them chatting to each other, just two of them, it sounded like. Again, we had to remain utterly still and silent. It was becoming all too clear to us that although we were travelling overland, through forests and across pasture, we were never going to be too far from people. That's how it was in rural Austria — tiny villages everywhere.

And sometimes it meant that we just had to be brazen. Late that afternoon, thirsty and in need of warmth, we decided to brew some tea. Carefully, we picked off a load of dried branches from the pine trees, knowing they wouldn't give off any telltale blue smoke as they burned. The woodcutting stopped. We reckoned that the cutters could smell the smoke, but they couldn't see it and were puzzled. Or perhaps they were having their own brew; who knows? Regardless, we made our cup of tea, and enjoyed it undisturbed. This was, for us, dining in style!

From where we sat, there among the pines, having our

cuppa, we had a great view, too, of the route ahead. In the distance, we could see a mountain range, a beautiful blue range rising up from the land of greys and greens. We knew that these were the Bacher Gebirge, the mountains that lie between Austria and Slovenia — our map told us so — and we were going to cross them. We figured that they were only about another fifteen miles away. One night's good walk away. One more small step in the plan, adding to the many we'd taken so far. With nods and whispers, we agreed: 'Tomorrow night, we should be there — we'll be in Slovenia.' It was an inspiring thought.

At nightfall, we headed off again, going for it flat out, but once again we lost the moon, as it disappeared into thicker and thicker cloud. Until now, the moon had been mostly on our left, reassuring us that we were going in the right direction — south. We'd navigated by measuring the angle between the moon and our compass bearing, and once we were on a setting we found that we did not have to look at the compass for pretty much the whole night. It was a crude method, but it worked. Not so well now, though.

It was pitch black, and some hours later we found ourselves smack up against a wall. A big one. What the hell was this? Silent and massive. We felt our way around the structure. It had to be a castle, and it was. In the first light of dawn its shadows took shape: a great medieval fortress, old, forbidding and with centuries of war behind it. This castle was strategically sited, as castles invariably are, on a ridge high above the Drau River, or the Drava, as it's called by Slavic peoples. But this particular castle, stopping us in our tracks as it did, had done us a favour: it had prevented us from tumbling down the steep slope of the ridge in the dark.

As the light began to brighten, we descended that slope carefully, knowing that a trip and a twisted ankle would be the end of us. We reached the bottom, and came across an old-fashioned sawmill, with a half-cut log lying across the pit, the blade of the saw still protruding from the wood. I thought of what a miserable job it would have been to stand in the pit, sawing away, with sawdust raining down on you — as the saying goes, that's the pits. Of course, the sawmiller would not have fancied being in my shoes at that time, either. The sawmill was deserted at that early hour, and we discussed whether we should hide out there for the day. It was dry and relatively comfortable. But I didn't fancy our chances if anyone came to work during the day.

So we climbed back up the hill and found a kind of lovers' nest about 200 yards above the mill, a natural, protected little rocky nook. From there, we could see out across the valley, although we could not see the river below. Over the other side, we could see a track and a train line, and throughout the day we heard trains chugging up and down the valley. A road of sorts, a railway line and a river: it was just as it looked on our map. And it meant we'd reached Slovenia.

Wkimedia Commons

The Bacher Gebirge — the mountain range between Austria and Slovenia. Pretty in this picture, but the mountains were still snowcapped when we crossed them in April.

We knew we would have to cross the river that night, and as we sat out the day in the nook, enjoying getting the sun into us, I contemplated my swimming prowess, or lack of it. So much for my relief a few weeks ago at not having to swim the Danube. While I might have done that spot of amateur surf-lifesaving back in Palestine, that was in water up to my knees. I really wasn't a strong swimmer at all. It would be fair to say that I was an adequate dog-paddler, who couldn't float: I sank like a stone if I tried. My river-swimming experience didn't go much beyond skinny-dipping in Musk Creek all those years ago at primary school. I wasn't confident I could swim the width of a road, let alone a freezing, rushing mountain river — in the dark.

13
GONE FERAL

But cross that river we would. We didn't have a choice. And the only way to cross it was to swim. Eric was the only experienced swimmer of the three of us, and fortunately, as it turned out, a very strong swimmer. Allan wasn't much more of a water baby than me, so any way we looked at it, this night was going to present a bit of a challenge.

We talked about it and decided to build a raft to carry our supplies. At about 10 p.m. we gathered bits of timber from the bank, and driftwood from the water — there was plenty of both — and tied them together with our belts and shoelaces. It was rough and ready, but so were we. We stripped naked and bundled our clothes and our stores of food together onto the raft. When we hit the water we could hear each other gasp. It was so cold it hurt. It was still only early spring, the river rose in the Alps and was full of snowmelt. I wouldn't recommend it.

In the darkness, I could see the mountains in the distance on the other side of the river, but I couldn't see the trees on the far bank. It looked a formidably long way across. Pretty quickly it occurred to me that it was not a river at all. It didn't have the feel of a stream; it didn't have a current. It seemed like a lake. I remember seeing little waves lapping at the shore: rivers don't do that. While the lack of current might have seemed an advantage, the thought that we were traversing a lake made me fearful about how far we had to go, and whether we were where we thought we were. I called out my concern to Eric, but he was reassuring: 'No — this is the river. We'll be right.'

Years later, when I met up with Eric again at home, he told me he'd worked out where we'd swum that night. This part of the river we were crossing was actually a weir built by prisoners en route from Greece to Central Europe. He'd been one of them. He said there were more wheelbarrows in that weir than in the whole of Australasia. Time and time again, the prisoners' wheelbarrows, loaded with cement, would 'accidentally' slip from their grip and fall into the water. The prisoners would then throw up their hands in mock despair at the German guards. It was their little way of sabotaging the German war effort. Eric did not know when we were there that night that it was the same weir — it was too dark to make out any landmarks that might have been familiar to him. He only realised after studying maps of the area when he got home.

We were in the water for at least an hour, and the cold was taking a toll. Allan and I were paddling along behind our loaded-up raft, and Eric was in front, pulling with a sturdy sidestroke. But halfway across, Allan said, 'I think I've got cramp.' I couldn't help him, I was struggling badly myself, seizing up in every muscle and numb with cold.

It was probably our salvation that the water was not running more strongly. We could now hear the roar of the water cascading over what we later knew to be the weir, and we understood plainly enough that we would be history if we allowed ourselves to be washed in that direction. It was Eric who was our saviour. 'I'll see how far it is,' he said, and swam off into the darkness. Ten or fifteen minutes later, he was back. 'It's not so far, we'll soon be there,' he said. 'Get stuck into it.' And we did. It seemed an eternity later that we pulled the raft up onto the far bank, exhausted.

And fairly devastated. The raft had proved to be a bit of a disaster. The driftwood we'd used was our near-fatal mistake: much of it was waterlogged, which meant that the raft had sat below the waterline, about six inches or so. Our clothes were sodden, and I'd seen several of our food parcels float away into the night. Now we were on land again — naked, freezing, hungry, and at severe risk of hypothermia. We jumped up and down, ran around, but our teeth were chattering so much we couldn't speak. We were in a state of shock. Suddenly my muscles didn't seem to be working at all; it was frightening. Allan and I weren't sure we could go on.

Eric volunteered to swim back across the river and go naked into a nearby town to ask for help. It was an heroic offer. He was as frozen as Allan and I, and there was no guarantee he would have made it back across the river. Nor could he have known what to expect from the villagers, wet and naked and unable to speak their language, in the middle of the night, in the middle of a war. It is amazing the reserves of courage a man can find in a moment like that. Months later, when this was all over, I'd write a letter recommending the award of a Victoria Cross to Eric for his heroism. Nearly fifty years later, Eric told me that the commanding officer who received it was impressed, but that he could not act on my recommendation — because I was only an NCO! Only an officer could recommend a soldier for a VC. That's the army for you. Eventually, Eric did end up with a medal — a Distinguished Conduct Medal — which was no less than his due.

As it happened, he didn't need to go back into the water that night. Allan recovered enough to start searching around the riverbank for firewood and soon found a tunnel, about four and a half feet in diameter, a perfect shelter. I thought at

AWM SUK13807

The countryside around Maribor, near the border of Austria and Slovenia.
It was always tempting to jump a train, but the risks were too great.
This train has taken a hit to the engine from an Allied bomber.

the time that it was a machine-gun post, but I think now it was probably dug to divert the water from the river while the coffer dams for the weir were being built. Anyway, it was a ready-made roof over our heads and protection from sight.

Together we gathered some dry leaves to start a fire. But our next misfortune was to find that the only box of matches we had was sopping wet, as was everything in Allan's haversack. He pulled out a match and tried to strike it, to no avail. Then ingenuity told. Allan, who liked a smoke, had that cigarette lighter. It was non-functioning now, but it still had its precious little store of fuel in it. Fingers working quick as his brain, he pulled the flint from the top of the lighter and poured some of the lighter fluid over the leaves. Then by striking the flint against a rock he managed to create a spark and got a fire going. Acutely aware of how vital this chance of warmth was for us, we carefully piled on more leaves and twigs, and soon we had a hell of a blaze. It saved our lives.

There was no effective outlet for the smoke in that tunnel, of course, so we sat there, still naked, half-blinded by smoke, tears streaming down our cheeks, but with hope renewed. We made a brew out of oatmeal and cocoa, which was pretty much all we had left. From having had a relatively good store of food, we now had so very little. I can't describe how devastating that fact was, but we couldn't afford to be miserable about it. We wrung out our clothes and hung them up on sticks to dry before the flames, incredibly grateful that we had not lost our clothes in the water as well. If we had, undoubtedly, it would have been all over for us. As we hung up our gear, we heard a train come down the line above the river. I looked up and saw the fireman stoking the boiler, shoving logs of wood into the firebox. Everything was wood-fired now: it seemed no-one in war-ravaged Europe had enough coal left to burn, or enough manpower to dig it out of the ground. It was an eerie moment, us with our fire, the fireman with his boiler, momentarily side-by-side in the lonely night. He must have wondered where all the smoke was coming from. They must have wondered in the town downstream, too. There was plenty of it.

~

Though we were warm and sheltered in that tunnel, we knew we couldn't stay there long. We were too vulnerable. Around 2 a.m., our uniforms still damp but no longer dripping, we set off again, climbing up the side of the valley. As dawn began to colour the sky, we found ourselves on a big, flat, rocky platform. It was a beautiful morning, clear and crisp, and from the rock we could see for miles across the timbered countryside. But it was also open and exposed. While we were lying there, a column of POWs passed by on the track immediately below us. We guessed later that they must have been from a big prison camp at Marburg, also called Maribor in Slovenian, which was not far away. They were probably being used as labourers on the railway line. As I peered down, one looked up. I dropped my head quickly, to avoid eye contact, and we lay dead still till they passed. The last thing we needed was for one of them to raise the alarm now. But if any of them saw us, clearly they said nothing about it.

The sun was bright now, so while we rested on the rock, we took off some of our clothes to get them more thoroughly dry in the sun. We also took stock of what remained of our supplies. All we had were some raisins and once dried — but now very soggy — biscuits. We agreed on a type of rationing: one raisin and a dried biscuit each, three times a day. That would constitute our meals. We put Allan in charge of carrying and distributing our few provisions. If he ate any more than Eric and I, we didn't know and didn't need to know.

We depended crucially on trust between ourselves. Early on in our escape, we had made Eric our mediator. It made sense: Allan and I were both Australians and sergeants; Eric was a New Zealander and a corporal. He was also a natural leader. If ever there was disagreement about, for instance, which way to go, Eric would choose, and we would abide by his choice. If it proved disastrous, we wouldn't blame him. We'd heard about other larger groups of escapees that ended up squabbling among themselves, or breaking up into smaller groups. Fatigue and stress could cause divisions and fights at the smallest provocation. We knew that unity would be vital for our survival. We knew we had to be steadfast.

Eric's casting vote came into play this morning. We had tried to climb up over a rocky embankment to find ourselves a more concealed position but it had proved futile. Allan clambered up first, then slipped down, bringing a mini-rockslide with him. Then I had a go but likewise tumbled back down, bringing lots of rubble with me, too. So we dusted ourselves down, abandoned that route and searched a bit further along the river valley slope until we came across a track going left and right. 'Your decision, Eric,' Allan and I said. Fortunately, he made a good one.

The path he chose took us into a wilder and less populated landscape; steep, rocky and heavily timbered. We walked on in daylight, more certain now that we would meet no-one in this back country, and as we continued to ascend, gradually rocks and timber gave way to snow. By nightfall, we were shin-deep in it. For several hours, we trudged on in silence, often slipping down through the snow, into loose piles of branches concealed underneath, the branches no doubt having been discarded by woodcutters. No-one wanted to say it, but the further we trudged, the more we were all thinking the same thing: what would we do at night? We weren't worried about running into anyone — the countryside was too remote for that — but we were very uncertain about where we would sleep. Still weak from last night's swimming expedition, we needed a warm place to get through this night, or hypothermia would have us for sure. We couldn't sleep in the open or we'd just plain freeze to death.

Suddenly, Lady Luck replied to our as yet unspoken concern, and we came upon an empty hut, probably the kipping spot for a shepherd or a forester. It was locked but we kicked the door down and again used Allan's cigarette lighter technique to start a fire in its little hearth. We nestled into each other and had the most comfortable night we'd spent in days.

At daybreak we set off again. The white of the snow was intense now, the wind blowing drifts into our faces, and of course none of us had protection for our eyes. It wasn't long before we all had snow blindness — eyes so blurry from the glare we couldn't read our map. Fortunately, we could still read the compass. We plodded on, saying little. Then after many hours, silent and hungry, we came over a ridge and began to descend. We were out of the worst of the snow and into thick forest. Distantly, we could hear a motorised sawmill working in a gully — that was a place to avoid.

We needed to rest, and luck smiled on us again, as not far off we found another shelter, a crude structure built of rough-hewn logs. I would say it was sleeping quarters for prisoners. There were no beds or blankets; more than likely, they slept back-to-belly, as we did. We searched around and in the rafters found some sugar and a needle. I imagine that there would have been a bit of a blue when the work party came back and found that their few supplies were gone.

That needle would prove more useful to us ragtag prisoners on the run. We used it to darn socks and patch up torn shorts, with threads of cotton pulled from other items. It was important to keep our clothes in the best repair we could manage, not only because we were determined to look respectable but because our uniforms were our essential protection from the elements. Our pants and shirts had been constantly wet for the past few days, and in the days and weeks to come they'd see more weather than this: we couldn't afford for them to rot. Our boots were the worst. After two days in the snow, mine were soft, just like two pieces of stewed meat. But somehow, they stayed intact.

Walking behind Allan and Eric, down through the forest earlier that day, I'd noticed something remarkable. Underfoot, they did not make a noise, no cracking of twigs, no rustling of leaves, no squeak of boots in the snow. They moved like wild animals do, or Indians, or Aborigines, padding soundlessly. They were not aware of it. If I'd felt a shift a few days before that, living wild as we were, and depending on our wits, developing the habits and instincts of animals, I knew it now. There we were, in the shelter, stealing a needle to darn our clothes, a tiny piece of human technology, but we'd gone feral.

~

Late in the afternoon, after trekking a few miles further, we needed to find shelter again and found it eventually in what looked like a little guard post. It was empty and we ducked inside, but the next thing we knew, we saw a German officer about fifty yards off coming down the track, skis slung over his shoulder. What's going to happen here, we thought to ourselves. The smoke from the fire we'd just built was curling up into the sky; it was obvious that there were people in the shelter. We didn't have time to concoct a story, and what would we say, anyway, to hoodwink a German officer? For all we knew he might have been coming to man this post. But he walked straight past us, and on down the track. We breathed a huge sigh of relief.

When darkness fell, we pulled our socks and squelchy boots back on and headed off down the track, following the German officer's footprints. There was still a fair bit of snow about, but there was a muddy path to follow. We hadn't been going long when we heard voices, growing ever louder as they came towards us up the track. Soon enough, a column of forty or fifty prison labourers with guards, by the sounds of it, passed us in the dark. Again, without exchanging a single word between us beforehand, Eric, Allan and I began to laugh heartily amongst ourselves in our 'German accents' as we walked, slapping each other on the back and exclaiming, 'Yah, yah,' making out that we were locals who had been up in the snow for the day.

Boldness be my friend, all right. Our ruse seemed to work, or maybe the German guards didn't care any more, too exhausted themselves. Just as well it was dark … We brushed past the bedraggled prisoners, who'd perhaps been working on the flats somewhere, or maybe labouring at a sawmill or something. They were probably Russian or French. They might even have been British. We would never know. This was not the time or the place for pleasantries.

We picked up the pace again and continued down the track. At the end of it, we could see an isolated building with

A lonely alpine hut. This isn't a picture of the Bacher Gebirge,
but it gives you an idea of the terrain we found ourselves in.
We really didn't have anywhere much to run and hide if spotted.

a blue light outside, indicating a police station. This was not
the place for us to be. To our left was another track, barred
with a rail preventing vehicles gaining access. Without a word
we turned left and slipped under the rail. Suddenly, a dog
emerged from the darkness and began to bark angrily at us.
We hurried on, shooing it away as we went, and thankfully it
shut up as we picked up our pace some more. By the time
anyone came out to see what the dog was making a fuss
about, we would have been well hidden in the night.

Eventually the track met a road heading south, in the
direction we wanted to go. We joined the road and were

trudging along when a big building loomed up out of the darkness. We approached it cautiously but with interest — we had to find somewhere to lie low during the day. It turned out to be a barn, a storage shed of some sort, for rural labourers probably, judging by the tools in there. We thought, this will do us. Inside, we felt secure, so we stayed there all the next day and the next night. The truth is that we were tired, sore, dirty and feverishly hungry — and unsure if we could go on. It wasn't despair, it was just that life on the run had taken its toll on our bodies and minds. We had two types of knots in our stomachs, one caused by hunger, the other by anxiety and tension. And we still had so far to go, to cross Slovenia and then …

We had almost run out of food entirely. During the second night, we snuck out into a field and dug up some carrots and cabbage stalks — any old piece of vegetable would do us. We'd kept a tin of salt; someone had told us that the body needed salt to stave off cramps and so as not to dehydrate as quickly. So we made a meal of carrots and salted cabbage stalks. It wasn't much. But it was better than nothing.

Over the two nights and a day in that barn, a kind of torpor took hold of us. We realised, despite our fatigued state of mind, that if we stayed there much longer, we would never leave. We had to press on. More than anything, we needed decent food — we were starving — so we set off along a track towards a distant village.

14
A LITTLE LUCK ON OUR SIDE

The next couple of days were a bit of a dazed scramble. We were still intent on making good our escape, but we were so ravenously hungry and we so badly needed to find food that we walked in broad daylight through what was now open countryside, with no forests to hide us. We didn't care much now about being seen or heard.

As we neared that first village, we met a bloke on a bicycle. '*Brot, brot?*' we pleaded with him, bread, bread. But he took one look at us and was off like a shot, not looking back even once — he didn't want to know anything about us. Nearer the village, a woman appeared on the veranda of her cottage and gestured for us to look ahead up the hill. We did as she indicated and there, in the midst of the line of twenty or twenty-five identical cottages, sat a more substantial building flying a giant swastika rippling in the sunlight. Almost certainly, the woman was trying to warn us of the German presence, gesturing for us to stay away or make a detour. But we were past caring. We marched on anyway, straight past the building with the flag. If anyone had looked out from the building, they could not have failed to see us. But no-one stopped us.

With less and less energy we kept going, eventually coming across a winery. There seemed to be nobody about, so we used our shoulders to push the door down. Inside, we found no food, but we did discover a detailed map of Croatia, the country that lay south of Slovenia — which would prove useful, if we ever made it beyond this winery. By now, we had nothing left to eat except a handful of raisins and a few dried biscuits. We were desperate, dizzy with hunger. Near the winery there was a farmhouse, with chooks running around in the yard. Allan and Eric began to hunt around for eggs, while I went inside to see what I could find. The kitchen was typical of those we'd seen already, simple but with plenty of farm produce. I stuffed my pockets with Spanish onions and was just about to dive into a big heap of figs soaking on a bench, when Allan called to me, 'You'd better come out — there's a lady coming up the track.'

She was indeed the lady of the house, of middle age, I suppose, coming back from the creek with her clean washing, and she was more curious than frightened as she approached us. In this time of war and massive upheaval, I suppose some of the locals had become accustomed to having strangers in tattered uniform from all over the place in their midst. We weren't so tattered yet, at least on the outside. She wanted to know who we were and what we were doing. We told her that we were German troops on leave. 'No, no, no,' she said. 'You're French, maybe?'

Anyway, Allan still had a cake of soap left in his haversack — we hadn't had an opportunity to use it ourselves yet — and soap, we knew, was a precious commodity in a place like this, and so he offered it to her in exchange for some food. To our relief, she obliged. Things were so desperate for these country people that soap — just a humble bar of ordinary scented soap — was a luxury. The lady brought out a little dish of maize, which had been soaked and cooked in a little enamel bowl. It was delicious. Then, to our amazement, she wanted to pay us for the soap, offering us some coins, which we refused. She insisted on giving us something, so she dug out some more Spanish onions. Her generosity was gratefully appreciated but baffling, till she told us a little of her story. Her husband was a Slovenian who had been conscripted into the German army, made an officer and sent away to the Russian front. It was a story we were to hear several more times: locals pressed into a cause they did not understand or care for. Remember, we were volunteers, not conscripts: we might have come to understand the disgrace of war, but we fully believed we were doing the right thing for the right cause; I still believe we did. But as that kindly woman spoke to us that day, and we realised that the building with the swastika aloft in the village was the recruiting station, it gave me pause for thought about the other side.

Duly, we went on our way, our hunger temporarily relieved. Not far off, we found an old bomb crater, possibly from World War I or early in this war, shaped like a pudding basin, around ten feet deep and grassed over. It made a natural hiding place. We climbed into it and ate the Spanish onions greedily. They were hot as hell — we had tears streaming down our faces and our mouths were on fire — but we didn't care. We were beggars, not choosers, and this was a precious commodity for us: a vegetable, with all its essential nutrition.

When we'd cleared the tears from our eyes, we pressed on, following a line of trees. We weren't using the compass now because it was daylight, but we were making an effort once again, now that we had some more energy, to try to keep ourselves from being spotted. We advanced using the natural features of the landscape for cover: the shadows of the trees and the breeze that stirred their branches and leaves. That day we followed the trees for hours, till it seemed we'd walked to the horizon and beyond. Eventually, we came across a house on stilts, with pigs and chooks scrabbling about underneath. There were also two teenage girls, maybe sixteen and eighteen, down there. They were in mud up to their knees, but they looked good to us: pink-cheeked, healthy country girls. We dared a fairly close look. We had all been away from home for a long time, at war, in prison camps, on the run, living only a semi-civilised existence — those girls looked lovely.

A middle-aged man came out of the house above — protective of his daughters no doubt — and wanted to know what we were doing. We muttered our usual lame story, that we were troops on leave, and he took us into his house. Again we thought we'd try to barter for some food. We gave him some ready-rubbed tobacco and a pair of sandshoes I had brought with us in case we needed to trade. He gave us cigarette papers; the cardboard slip had a picture of a flag on it, one I didn't know. Then he got out a big enamel dish and cooked up some small chat potatoes, skins and all, which he had probably been keeping for the pigs, and stirred in some bacon fat for flavour. We ate the lot with relish. Again, we had cause to marvel at the generosity of these country folk, who took risks with their own safety to help us.

I couldn't believe then — and still can't now — how miserably poor most of those villagers were, and how they managed to survive two wars. They had only what they grew or manufactured for themselves. They made their own cheese, fattened their own pigs with the waste, made bacon from the pigs, and cured the bacon to store up for winter, perhaps picked a few grapes for wine in summer — and they shared what they had. It's amazing to think that Germany ever believed they could win the war when this was what was going on in the lives of ordinary people. In war, the army gets everything: the men, the best of the farm produce, the best wool for uniforms and blankets, the coal to make and transport their weapons of destruction; while the people get little at all. At home in Australia, not that we knew it at the time, you couldn't buy pork — because it was all sent off to the United States army, for tins of pork and beans for its soldiers. It hit home here, though, in the Slovenian countryside, what an utter waste war is. We were so grateful for the generosity of these people; we knew they couldn't afford to spare much. We would not have survived without the trust and simple human kindness of these poor farming people of Austria and Slovenia.

We left the house on stilts and moved on into heavily timbered country. As before, we continued to risk walking during the daylight, as the nights remained overcast and moonless. We walked and walked, until we came to a railway line, and there, tired to the bone, we considered waiting to jump a train. It was a common tactic for escapees but dangerous: the trains were stoutly guarded. Another problem was that we didn't know where the railway line led. In the end, we decided against it. While we were resting on a trail that ran up to the railway line, two kids came by, a boy and a girl, aged barely ten, dressed in the scouts-type uniform of the

Air Force Historical Research Agency

The quaintly dilapidated farmhouses of this region make nice postcards today, but the poverty of those farming families who lived in them shocked me during our flight. The war took so much from ordinary country folk.

Hitler Youth — the next generation being trained for the insane ambitions of the Third Reich, I thought. It made us realise that we were still far from out of danger. If they had decided to kick up a fuss, there would have been nowhere for us to run. But they walked by; just kids, interested in whatever they were doing, not in us.

Before we could get away from this exposed place, an elderly man came along. From beneath his cloth cap, he looked at us and asked who we were. As usual, we gave him the story that we were German troops on leave. 'No, you're French,' he retorted. 'Actually, Australians,' we said. With nowhere to run, and him being just an old man, there seemed no point keeping up any pretence. But our answer stumped him. 'Austrian?' he asked quizzically. I doubt that he had even heard of Australia. We asked him if he had any bread, and he said he'd go back to see what he could find.

We were committed to staying where we were now. Next, a lone soldier in a German uniform turned up, carrying a rifle. Immediately we could see he wasn't threatening. We fell into conversation, in cobbled-together German and English, and he told us he was a local, a Slovenian, another conscript who was being packed off to the Russian front. 'Well, why don't you come with us?' we asked. He looked at us glumly. 'I can't,' he said, and explained that the Germans would come back and burn down his house, and cart his family off to a concentration camp if he did. This was the gruesome threat that kept all these reluctant conscripts in line. Again it was amazing to me to think that Germany believed it could win a war with half their soldiers 'recruited' in such a way. No loyalty, no heart for it.

Later, an old lady, the wife of the old man who'd chatted to us earlier, came back with a loaf of bread. Boy, did we hop into that! How long had it been since we'd had fresh bread? And it was beautiful bread, tasty, a scone loaf, sweet and grainy, packed with sustenance. It was manna from heaven.

~

Luck, guesswork and our survival instincts had taken us a long way. Now, dimly, we began to understand how far. The old lady who'd brought us the bread kept saying to us: 'Grenze, Grenze.' She was frantic. We had no idea what she was talking about. We looked at our map, and sure enough we found 'Grenze' on it, right on the border between Slovenia and Croatia — we'd had no idea that *Grenze* was the border itself, that that was the word in German. But it was clear enough where we were: between a rock and a hard place: between Slovenia, which was occupied by Germany, and Croatia, which was in the hands of the murderous Ustashi — right-wing extremists whose atrocities horrified even the Nazis. It was a border that was likely to be heavily guarded, and crossing it would be our greatest challenge.

We waited for darkness to fall, then pressed on down the track from the railway line. Again that night, we slept back-to-belly, in the refuge of a clump of trees. When we woke the next morning, we could see that we were in the lee of a high ridge. In the half-dark, I looked up and spotted something that made my blood run cold. I crawled over to Eric, who was combing his hair, and whispered, 'Look up, but not too quickly.' He did and saw what I had seen: a guard in a German helmet patrolling the top of the ridge above us, only about a hundred yards away. He was looking not directly down at us, but out across the valley below. This was indeed the border.

We alerted Allan, and then we spied another German guard coming from the other direction along the ridge.

Between them was a thicket of pine trees, which they seemed to be keeping under particular surveillance. We waited until they had crossed paths and their backs were turned, then scrambled deeper into our copse, into the bushy undergrowth. It was still early morning; the sun was just rising. We lay there for hours, not speaking, not moving, hardly daring to breathe. I suppose we were petrified; my mind and my heart were certainly racing. Somehow, we had to get across this border to continue our journey south, but we didn't know how well it was guarded, nor how dangerous it would be on the other side.

Towards the bottom of the valley, further down right below us, we could see a farmer driving a horse and plough over his field. From our hide-out in the pine trees, we could see the horse's head and ears as he came closest to us. Each time, the horse would look at our pines and prick up his ears. He knew we were there — fortunately, no other living creature did.

It was nature that would come to our aid. About one or two in the afternoon, the sky clouded over, black as hell, and a mighty rainstorm burst down on us, drenching us and driving everyone else indoors, including the guards. It only lasted five or ten minutes, but it was enough. This was our opportunity and we seized it. We scrambled out of the trees, into the rain and over the top of the ridge. We had no idea of what to expect on the other side, but we knew that that was where we had to go — at the fastest sprint we could muster.

A young German guard.
He looks so young —
we all were.

Over the ridge was a deep valley of open green grasslands, sloping away to a watercourse — a river or canal — bordered by a barbed-wire fence. A large group of peasant labourers, fifty or sixty, were trudging along in the rain on a track next to the channel. They had probably been working further up the valley, and were returning to their homes now that the storm had set in. With barely a word, we fell in with them.

It was a surreal moment. We spread ourselves out among the workers so as not to be too obvious. We didn't look back, even once, for that would also have been a giveaway. We did as the others did, clumping along in the mud, to avoid raising suspicions. None of the labourers said anything. None alerted the guards, high on the hills above us. I can only presume that they were no more fond of the Germans than we were. After all, the Germans were occupying *their* country and for all we knew might have been forcing them to work to produce food for an army they didn't consider to be on their side.

But the men were nervous, too, giving us sly glances. They knew that if any guards along the top of the ridges spotted us the bullets would start flying. They weren't soldiers like us and they had no protection. They didn't want to be caught in the middle. We were a danger to everyone. All we were carrying by then was a few scraps of begged vegetables, but if the Germans had caught us, I'm sure they would have beaten us to learn the identities of our benefactors. Almost anything we said under duress would have led to danger for someone else — even just letting the Germans know what villages we'd passed through. I suspected such brutality at the time, and I knew that Eric had been belted in military prison for simply going for a ramble among the blackberries, but it wasn't until after the war that the world would know just how brutal the SS and Gestapo were. On the Croatian side of the border, it would have been even worse — the Ustashi made the SS and Gestapo look like pussycats. It was probably just as well we were largely ignorant of that at the time, too!

Slowly, the ranks of peasant workers thinned, as they filed off to their homes, until it was nearing the point when we would be the only men left. What happened next shows how mentally attuned to one another we had become during our adventures. The path we were following lay beside an expanse of apron wire — a barrier of coiled barbed wire strung along the water channel. Between the path and the wire, hard up against it, was a pile of mulchy leaves, about two feet high, just like the pile that had come to our rescue on our very first day on the run. As one, the three of us flopped into the leaves and within seconds had covered ourselves. This sort of thing happened time and time again, as if by telepathy, without a word passing between us, we would all know what needed to be done in that moment. Any hesitation could have been fatal.

We stayed hidden in those leaves until about 9 or 10 p.m. that night, never stirring, never talking, just lying there. We knew our lives depended on it. Our next move would be to get under the barbed wire and — somehow — across the canal, but it would have to wait until dark, absolute dark, and late enough, we hoped, for the guards' alertness to be dimmed. It was again a long, damp, cold wait.

All along the wire were signs reading: '*Minen*', indicating, supposedly, that the whole of the barbed-wire fence was laid with mines. I had a hunch that the Germans would not have bothered to mine the entire area of the apron wire fence, twenty-five feet thick and who knows how many miles long. They needed the mines for the Russian front and other theatres of war. It would have been cheaper and more sensible

The type of sign that was strung along the wire by the canal.

to put up signs warning of mines, the way people put stickers on their house windows nowadays warning of nonexistent security systems. It was a kind of bluff, I was sure. In any case, we could not go back now. We had no choice but to back my hunch.

We knew how to get under barbed wire; the army had trained us for that. This type of apron wire was configured like a lace net of crisscrossing coils, four or five feet in height and so dense there was no chance you could walk through it — unless you blew it up first. Still covered by the heap of leaves, we rolled onto our backs and began to pull ourselves under the mesh of wire, one strand at a time. Our few possessions we would push ahead of us and pick up as we inched our way through. It was slow going, through twenty-five feet of this stuff. Frequently, one or other of us would become snarled on the wire and have to disentangle himself. It meant plenty of scratches on hands and faces, and lots of muttered curses. But we persevered; had to.

Oddly enough, while we were inching our way beneath the wire on our backs, we heard a voice start to sing, a woman's voice. Then another joined hers, harmonising. The singing seemed to be coming from a hill not more than half a mile away above us, and soon there were many voices, a whole choir of them: women singing a round that sounded like a hymn, all in harmony, filling the valley with their song. It was indescribably beautiful. There I was, so far away from home, cold, hungry and with a face full of barbed wire, and I was thinking, what a wonderful world!

I've always liked to believe that those women sang their song that night because their men had gone home and told them about the three foreign soldiers they'd seen that day. They had guessed what we were up to, perhaps had even been watching us, and had decided to distract the Germans with a communal effort. I will never know if that was true or not, but it's a wonderful thought.

Finally, blessedly, we were free of the wire and at the edge of the canal. We were still making plans on the run. This canal was about fifteen yards wide, and as far as we could tell by jabbing a long stick into it, five or six feet deep — and mountain-water cold. We would have tried to swim it, as we had swum the Drava, but Eric had been sickening for a few days, since we'd been through the snow, and now, after our long, damp wait this night, he suddenly had a cold so bad he could hardly talk. Entering that water might have killed him. Instead, we decided to walk along the bank. In the pitch dark, even that was hazardous. Eric led as we felt our way along. Every so often, he would warn us about tripwires coming up, which were tied to wooden stays driven in the bank, thus tensioning the barbed-wire fence.

At length, we came to a bridge. On our side, the Slovenian side, there was a guardhouse with a light on inside it — a sort of one-man prefabricated box, like an outside dunny, which you'd see everywhere. We watched for a while, waiting to see a movement or a shadow cross the small window of the thing, hardly breathing, then concluded that there was no-one in there. So, carefully, we climbed the barbed wire that was strung from the bottom of the canal to the bridge rail — which was about ten feet high here, and easy to scale — then we tumbled down the other side onto the bridge. We paused for a moment, listening for the sound of an alarm. There was none, just the deafening silence of the night. Anxious about the noise our boots might make on the timber boards, we took them off and padded across the bridge.

On the other side, as we were putting our boots back on, Allan stopped and hissed, 'There's two sentries over there.' So there were, shadowy figures under the shelter of some trees about a hundred yards away. Strangely, you can sort of see in the dark if you spend enough time in it, and our night vision had become acute, enough to recognise shapes in the black against the black night world. Then, a heartbeat afterwards, Eric hissed, 'And here comes the bloody dog.' A big Alsatian was bounding flat out towards us, lips curled, eyes shining in the dark. Our hearts sank into our shabby boots. All this way, all the fatigue, all the privations, all the risk, all the times we thought we were done for, and it would come to nought. Humans we could fool, but a guard dog?

We crouched in the shadows of the bridge. Eric cursed the dog fiercely, snarling at him under his breath, calling him a mongrel and a cur and a few other nastier New Zealand words. The dog looked at us, and for a moment, time stood still. Suddenly, it turned and ran back to its handlers as quickly as it had come at us, as if it had been taking lessons in Kiwi profanities. It didn't bark and, incredibly, the sentries appeared none the wiser.

I can't explain why or how that dog left us alone. Perhaps it was because we stayed low, crouching and flattening ourselves on the ground, and that confused the dog. If we had been standing, he would have jumped all over us, I'm certain of that. Perhaps it was because by this time we hadn't had a wash for over a week. Almost certainly, the guards didn't wash much, either; this was a remote outpost. Probably, to the dog, we smelled just like them. Maybe we all smelled more animal than human. Whatever the reason, the dog obviously could not tell if we were friend, foe or civilian. Again, fortune had smiled upon us.

Eventually, the guards did come, but by then we had scarpered off into a crop of oats as high as our heads. We were pretty certain the guards would not follow us, even if they had seen us. They would not have known who we were and what we might do to them. They were probably conscripts anyway, forced to do a miserable job, with no heart for it, and would have been quite happy to say that they had seen and heard nothing all night.

When the sun rose again the next morning we were well into Croatia, by at least five miles. It was April 20, 1944 — twelve days since we had fled Petzendorf. Miraculously, we were still free.

15
LOST IN CROATIA

We knew we were in Croatia, but had no way of knowing whether that would be better or worse for us than Austria or Slovenia had been. We were still heading south, still with the idea of reaching the Adriatic coast, perhaps stealing a boat and — if necessary — rowing across to Italy. If not, there was the possibility we would link up with the Partisans, the Yugoslav resistance, militants who were loosely on our side, fighting the Germans and the Ustashi, in their own war against fascism. Perhaps they'd help us reach our mob. We'd heard about their activities in the Balkans from listening to the BBC back in Spittal. But our priority at this moment was to eat. We were completely out of food by now, famished and exhausted.

In the light of dawn, we could see a big hill rising up before us. It was lush and green, a marvellous sight, and just like the country near my home in Gippsland. I half expected to see the dairy cows I used to mind grazing there. A landscape to make you want to hop on a horse and go for a long ride — if you weren't really a POW on the run with no idea where to next. Allan, Eric and I discussed which side of the hill we would tackle — left or right. I remembered the lesson I had learned from Major Gwynne in Palestine at the beginning of my war. He had put such a dilemma to us: there is a hill in front of you, with machine guns on each side at the bottom. Which way to attack? Some had said one way, some the other. I had suggested that we train guns on both enemy positions simultaneously and attack straight over the top. Major Gwynne liked it: later, he recommended me for further training as an NCO. Now that training came to the fore. There were no machine guns here, as far as we could tell, but there was a lot of unknown. With little hesitation, we marched straight up the hill, and no obstacle met us on our way.

At the top, we found a dirt track leading away to a forest. We were just about to head down it when I saw a house nearby. I decided to throw caution to the wind. We hadn't eaten anything of substance since the old lady's loaf of bread three days before. 'I'm going down there to get some food,' I said.

I sped straight down to that house and knocked on the door. An old bloke answered. I can't imagine what he must have thought. I would have looked a sight: unshaven and unwashed for days, clothing tattered and torn, desperately tired, scratches and scrapes all over me, and probably with that hollow look around the eyes that starving people get. I must have given him a hell of a shock. And I couldn't speak his language, of course. I tried to use sign language to explain myself. But he took fright: he stepped out his door and slammed it shut behind him. Then he started waving his hands, seeming to indicate for me to wait where I was before he disappeared at a run down the track.

I sat down on the doorstep, unable to go on. Allan and Eric, who'd been watching from about twenty yards off, came over to me and asked me what I reckoned was going on. 'It doesn't look too good,' I said. 'It looks like we're going back to the barbed wire.' I was resigned to returning to prison camp at that moment; resigned to interrogations, a beating in the military prison, and failure. Without food, we couldn't continue, and we all knew it. A silence came over us. It made for a glum mood, to say the least.

The Croatian householder was gone for about twenty minutes. Next thing, two soldiers came around the corner, rifles at the ready. But instead of the uniforms of the SS or the dreaded Ustashi, they were wearing plain caps with no peak, sporting the red star of communism. These, we knew immediately, were Partisans: the Yugoslav resistance fighters. We could have hugged them. Perhaps we did.

~

Our luck had held — just. We had no idea of the odds of running into Partisans rather than Ustashi, but, boy, were we glad we did.

We exchanged greetings as best we could with our rescuers, who took us to another house, owned by an Austrian Partisan who could speak English. He told us we were in a village called Krapina, and gave us some stew and an apple each. We gulped the food down. Meanwhile, the Partisans were watching us closely, suspiciously, and who could blame them? They thought that we might have been planted by the Germans, to infiltrate their group. The fact that we were wearing British uniforms seemed only to make them more paranoid. We didn't know why. The Austrian put a Luger on the table and said in an ominous voice, 'If you're not who you say you are, you'll be executed. Understand?'

Yes, we did. And, as we'd learn, the Partisans didn't take prisoners. Since they were constantly on the move, they couldn't afford to carry captives around with them. Nor could they afford the risk of a prisoner escaping. They depended on the element of surprise. An ex-prisoner with knowledge of their hide-outs and movements could deny them that. They were still few in number and could be wiped out quickly if they were not disciplined and vigilant. So their policy was old and simple: dead men don't tell tales. Whatever prisoners they did take, they executed at the first opportunity.

The Partisans used a radio phone to contact Australia House in London. We'd given them our parents' names, army numbers, regiments, the usual identifying information. By day's end, they had verified us. They knew we were okay — so would Australia House, we hoped. One Partisan officer, a big, bearded bloke with bandoliers of bullets around his waist and grenades on his hips, wanted to know how we had gotten through the wire and whether we had shot anyone. Details mattered, and so did looting corpses of anything and everything that was useful. As we'd also come to learn, when

Corbis U725516ACME

A Partisan headquarters well hidden and guarded in a steep gully. We were so lucky to have stumbled across Partisans rather than Ustashi.

the Partisans were short of clothes, they would ambush and shoot a German soldier on the border, taking care to put the bullet through the head so as not to ruin the uniform! This probably also explained why the German guards at the bridge might not have wanted to chase us.

In the evening, the Partisans took us to another building in Krapina to sleep. It was pretty primitive. There were no beds or blankets, just some straw on the ground, but we were grateful for whatever we got; it looked like the Hilton to us. We fell into the deepest sleep imaginable, not just from exhaustion, but because at last we were safe — or at least the safest that we'd been in what seemed an age. But during the night, the door was suddenly flung open and a Partisan officer came in, holding a gun to the head of a youth. The poor kid was shaking with terror. It was explained to us later that the boy had fallen asleep under a tree when he was supposed to be on sentry duty, and the officer told him he would be shot next time. I'm not sure, but I think it might have been for our benefit — a show of the officer's authority and the kind of discipline he meted out. An unnecessary show, though. We weren't going to cause any trouble. All we were interested in was continuing our journey south, to freedom.

~

Croatia at that time was a country of outlaws. The Ustashi were officially in charge, but theirs was a reign of terror, responsible for the deaths of at least 450,000 Serbs, Gypsies, Jews and dissidents in concentration camps — the total number they murdered in their holocaust will never be known. We knew very little of this at the time, but across the country there were all manner of refugees — political, racial, and Allied escapees like us. Some had fled from prison camps in Austria, others had jumped from prison trains making their way up from Greece a few years ago. Most of these itinerants, soldiers and citizens, linked up with the Partisans at some stage in their journeys. Knowing this, the British had sent liaison officers into the Balkans, establishing missions to give heart and strength, but especially arms, to the Partisans, for every blow they struck against the Ustashi and against Germany was a blow for the cause of the Allies. The liaison officers also worked to repatriate escapees across the Adriatic to Italy — and that's what we were after. And it was the reason why we were more or less looked after by the Partisans — because the more Allied soldiers they handed over to the British, the more arms they got in return.

Perhaps reflecting thousands of years of shifting alliances and political turmoil in the Balkan peninsula, the Yugoslav resistance militias were themselves divided. Some were under the command of General Drazha Michailovic, a Serbian royalist; others were under General Josip Tito, a Croat and a

Firemen of the Drouin Brigade.
Me on the left with my mate
Hughie Spencer.

Our Drouin football team, well before the war. I'm in the back row, fourth from the left.
The bloke on my left, Dave Kelton, was killed at Tobruk. Another mate, Ted Gould, third from
the right, ended up in New Guinea.

My good mate Jack Walsh, on the left, the day he came to visit me in Palestine for my 21st birthday.

German propaganda leaflet dropped over Tobruk — we used them for toilet paper.

AUSSIES

AFTER CRETE DISASTER ANZAC TROOPS ARE NOW BEING RUTHLESSLY SACRIFICED BY ENGLAND IN TOBRUCH AND SYRIA.

TURKEY HAS CONCLUDED PACT OF FRIENDSHIP WITH GERMANY. ENGLAND WILL SHORTLY BE DRIVEN OUT OF THE MEDITERRANEAN. OFFENSIVE FROM EGYPT TO RELIEVE YOU TOTALLY SMASHED

YOU CANNOT ESCAPE.

OUR DIVE BOMBERS ARE WAITING TO SINK YOUR TRANSPORTS. THINK OF YOUR FUTURE AND YOUR PEOPLE AT HOME.

COME FORWARD - SHOW WHITE FLAGS AND YOU WILL BE OUT OF DANGER !

SURRENDER !

Mark Mawson Photography

ABOVE My old slouch hat. The 'T' badge on the band denotes that I was at Tobruk.
BELOW My dogtags, with my blood group and service number — VX17575 — written on them.
There's a couple of Lebanese coins strung with them as souvenirs, too. The square tag here is
my POW tag, from Stalag 18A/Z.

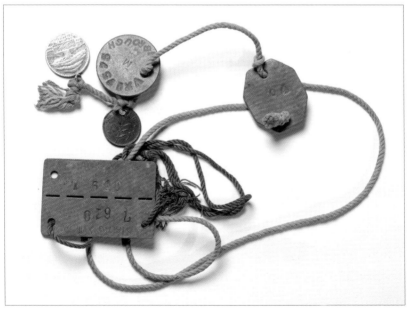

Mark Mawson Photography

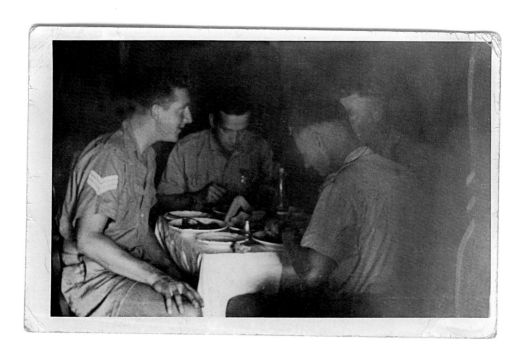

ABOVE Tucking into steak and eggs on leave in Tel Aviv, 1941.

Services Guide to Cairo

PUBLISHED BY THE
CO-ORDINATING COUNCIL
FOR WELFARE WORK IN EGYPT.

We were given these guides to Cairo on leave between Tokruk and El Alamein.

The cherished Partisan cap given
to me by Puks Boris in Croatia.

The citation I received for the award of the Military Medal.

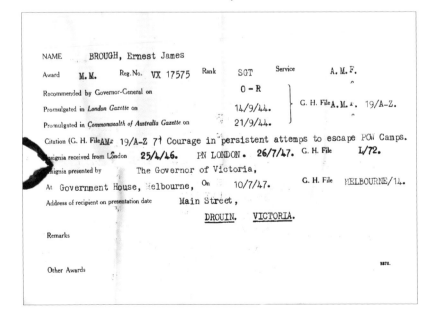

NAME   BROUGH, Ernest James

Award   M.M.   Reg.No. VX 17575   Rank   SGT   Service   A. M. F.

Recommended by Governor-General on   O - R

Promulgated in *London Gazette* on   14/9/44.   G. H. File A. M. F.   19/A-Z.

Promulgated in *Commonwealth of Australia Gazette* on   21/9/44.

Citation (G. H. File AMr 19/A-Z 7† Courage in persistent attemps to escape POW Camps.

Insignia received from London   25/4/46.   PN LONDON. 26/7/47.   G. H. File   L/72.

Insignia presented by   The Governor of Victoria,

At Government House, Melbourne, On   10/7/47.   G. H. File   MELBOURNE/14.

Address of recipient on presentation date   Main Street,

                              DROUIN.   VICTORIA.

Remarks

Other Awards   3576.

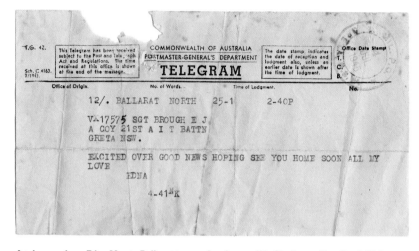

Office of Origin.   No. of Words.   Time of Lodgment.   No.

12/. BALLARAT NORTH   25-1   2-40P

VA17575 SGT BROUGH E J
A COY 21ST A I T BATTN
GRETA NSW.

EXCITED OVER GOOD NEWS HOPING SEE YOU HOME SOON ALL MY
LOVE
      EDNA

4-41NK

A telegram from Edna May in Ballarat to me when I was off in Singleton, New South Wales, after deciding I'd had enough of the army.

Edna May and Ernest James Brough, proprietors of the 'Most Modern Butcher's Shop in Victoria'. They were great days.

E. J. & E. M. BROUGH
QUALITY BUTCHERS
MYER ST., LAKES ENTRANCE

WISH TO ANNOUNCE THAT THEY WILL BE OPEN

For friendly trading on the morning of

AUGUST 4, 1959

. . in the . .

MOST MODERN BUTCHER'S SHOP
IN VICTORIA

All our Meat is Personally selected and Slaughtered under Government supervision at Hayward's Abattoirs, Bairnsdale

It is Delivered to our Premises in an up-to-date Meat Van

All our Meat is Top Quality

Our Prices are Right

And Service is Supreme

JAMES YEATES AND SONS PTY. LTD.

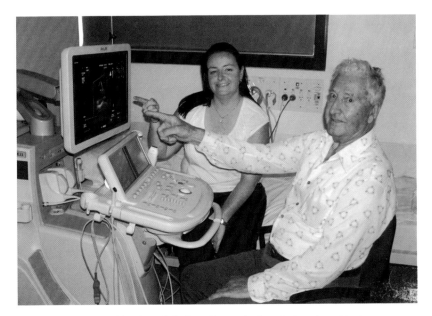

Me and my eldest granddaughter, Sally Anne Cooper, having a look at that whizz-bang heart machine.

A bunch of old soldiers with a couple of kids from Belmont High, Geelong, when we presented the school with a Rats of Tobruk flag. Artie Byrns, who enjoys remembering exactly where I was shot, is in the very centre of the photo.

Photo by Phillip Stubbs, Geelong Advertiser

In my element, at the Colac sale yards, inspecting cattle.

Me and Artie Byrns at our favourite haunt, Geelong RSL.

communist. Tito, later to become president of a united Yugoslavia, was anti-Nazi and anti-fascist and demanded all-out resistance, so he was a natural ally for the Allies. The Allies initially had armed both bands of resistance fighters, but as they became more and more suspicious of Michailovic's apparent reluctance to fight Germany, they concentrated their attention and largesse on Tito. The lot we had landed ourselves with were, fortunately, Tito's Partisans.

We gathered that this contingent of Partisans had been in the north of Croatia on a recruiting mission. Now, the following morning, they were leaving Krapina, in a long column of about three hundred, including us, and we began to wend our way east through the wilds of northern Croatia to continue whatever their mission was. East wasn't exactly the direction we wanted to go, but again, beggars couldn't be choosers.

It was an expedition only for the hardy. We travelled light, to say the least. We had a couple of mules to carry ammunition and machine guns, but no artillery or tanks, of course. The Partisans all carried grenades and guns, but Eric, Allan and I were unarmed: they didn't trust us enough for that. Instead, we carried ammunition, typewriters and other supplies, but little or no food. I'm not sure even now how the Partisans sustained themselves. As we travelled, here and there we would find little rounds of sour milk — like cottage-cheese cakes — hundreds of them on the gateposts of

Corbis U98324INP

These Yugoslav school kids, some wearing the red star of the Partisans, show in their smiles the people's hopes of liberation from war and fascism. Us escapees on the run would often be greeted with the same enthusiasm by villagers in Croatia.

sympathisers, which saved the Partisans the bother of having to go into houses to beg for food. We would get one or two of these a day, if we were lucky.

There were no meal breaks, no regular meal times. Sometimes we would go two or three days without eating at all. But the Partisans, though rough and sometimes callous, could be unexpectedly kind. Once, one of them asked if we were hungry. 'Yes,' we replied, nearly screeching. He produced a four-pound bag full of hot white bread, as well as jam. It made for a hearty meal. Another time, a Partisan took pity on us and showed us to a house for breakfast. There we were lavished with meat, soup, eggs, hot milk and porridge with cream, and more beautiful bread. The old lady who owned the house made us eat until the buttons were almost popping off our jackets. Since this was our first decent meal for days, we didn't need much encouragement. But that was how it tended to be: feast or famine, nothing in between.

We learned to take what we could get and be grateful. One night, we were half-asleep in a pigsty somewhere when that big, black-bearded Partisan lieutenant suddenly burst in, double bandolier of bullets glinting across his chest. He told us to hold out our hands, which he filled with yellow rock salt. Weird meal, yes, and it tasted strangely sweet. Next, he filled our cupped hands with sugar. We ate greedily. There were no eating utensils; it was bare hands or nothing. Another night, the caravan stopped in a sympathetic neighbourhood, quite a large village or small town, and the Partisans, including us, went off in little groups of six to a house. Dogs barked as we neared the house we'd be stopping in, but our comrades glared at them and told them to shut up. There were people inside the house and sentries posted outside, but more importantly for us, there was a small enamel washbasin holding about a gallon of milk, with bread broken up in it. We were given a spoon each, and I quickly understood: this was survival of the fittest. Whoever ate the most would last the longest. So there we were, six ravenous fugitives, greedily eating out of one dish.

We travelled at night or in the early morning, up and down mountains, getting caked to the shins in mud and chilled to the bone. The Partisans posted scouts on the hills and ridges, but stuck mostly to the valleys as they moved. There we were not so visible, either to the Ustashi or to German planes, which could get at us only by flying dangerously low into the trees. Frequently, the rain was pouring down and there was a driving wind in our faces, but we pressed on. During the day, we would rest up, sometimes in the farmhouses of sympathisers, sometimes in the forest. We found we had one thing in common with the Partisans: in the wild, they slept as we had in Austria and Slovenia, back-to-belly. I saw up to thirty of them pressed together in this highly heat-efficient way.

It was a nomadic, edgy, Spartan existence, much as you would imagine it is for rebels or terrorists on the run now. But the mood of the travelling party was spirited. At stops the

Partisans would play guitars and sing great impromptu concerts while waiting for their scouts to report back. They were remarkable in the way they could be half-starving, living a life of constant tension, and then break into these rousing tunes, full of laughs and wild strumming of guitars. I don't know what they were singing about — probably songs of revolution or their equivalent of smutty soldiers' ditties — but duly, we learned to sing along with them, sort of. Looking back, I wonder if we were in Croatia or in a crazy spaghetti western somewhere in Mexico.

All the while, Eric, Allan and I had a constant companion, a Yugoslav called Madic, pronounced Maditch — we dubbed him Ted McDitch. He could speak good English, and rarely left our side, but he said nothing to us, ever. We'd goad him: 'Come on, can't you talk?' or 'Can't you just buzz off and leave us alone?' Doubtless he was our Partisan chaperone, posted to listen in on all our conversations and report back to command. The only time he did leave us for those first four or five weeks was to go on what appeared to be scouting missions into this village or that. He wore plain civilian dress and a black beret; I'm sure he was a spy of some sort, checking us out, and slipping quietly in and out of those villages. But we'd never know. One day, near the end of our time with the Partisans, he simply disappeared altogether.

It became clear to us that the Partisans were fighting not only the Nazis and the Ustashi; they were fighting anyone and everyone not on the side of their cause. And they could be brutal about it; there is no other way to say it. Early on the morning of our third day travelling with them, around 4 a.m., they raided a big village called Ivanec. They didn't take us with them, since we were unarmed. But we could hear bullets whistling, ricocheting and echoing in the morning stillness. Later, a Partisan guide took us into the town. We saw pillboxes that had been blown apart to drive out the enemy. We saw a small tank that had been captured; published photographs of it would become the talk of Croatia for weeks. A dead Ustashi soldier was still lying on the street near the tank, while children played nearby and women walked past obliviously. It showed how hard years of war had made these people. But on learning we were Allied soldiers, they all wanted to know who we were, where we had been and what we knew. They were also very excited to see a flight of American bombers pass overhead, bound for Germany. So were we.

The Partisans had no time for compassion. They dragooned men into their party and threatened to shoot anyone who refused. They told us later they had killed 140 enemy troops at Ivanec and taken many prisoners, whose future was grim. But it was a lightning raid. The Partisans knew not to stay long in case a German tank or an artillery gun was nearby. Just as they could not afford to keep prisoners, nor could they afford casualties. There were no hospitals and little in the way of medical supplies to help the wounded. The stark primitiveness of this conflict reminded me in some ways of what I had read about the American Civil War, and brutality and speed being the key to victory.

Tag-along escapees like us had our use that day at Ivanec, too. As a grisly silence settled over the town, one of the Partisans told us to go up to the bakery and take what bread we could there. So the three of us did. We took a loaf each, but that didn't look to be enough. This moment called for ingenuity. I was wearing a pair of John L. Sullivan long johns, as supplied by the Red Cross back in Spittal. They hadn't been washed in three weeks but that didn't matter now. I dropped my tweeds, took off the long johns and tied a knot in the bottom of each leg. Then we filled them with loaves of bread, like a sack. The underwear stretched, of course, but we must have ended up with at least half a dozen loaves of bread in each leg. I slung them over my back, put my trousers back on and away we went. Unfortunately, once the bread all disappeared, so did my old faithful long johns.

We moved on, back into wild country, and the next night we came across an abandoned mansion in the forest. We lit a fire inside and turned our ration of that bread into toast. In the morning we woke to beautiful sunny weather and Eric, Allan and I had a chance to wash our clothes thoroughly for the first time in fifteen days. We killed as many lice as we could on ourselves and in the seams of our clothes, and sunbathed until we were red raw. Sunburn never felt so good.

At one point earlier in our journey with the Partisans we had even got a chance to luxuriate in a thermal spring. It was an outdoor communal bath, only about three feet deep but, ahhhhh, that warm water was the loveliest thing that had touched our skins in a very, very long time. We stayed in there for half an hour, at least, and would have stayed longer if we hadn't been told to get out because an enemy tank was heading our way. We could hear guns distantly pounding through the air, so it was time to move on. Twenty years later, in Perth, Allan would be stopped by a Yugoslav immigrant on a tram, who said, 'I know you, from Croatia,' and it turned out that he had shared the bath with us that day. Small world!

It was an intensely violent world in Croatia at the time, though, and we continued to turn a blind eye to the cruelty we witnessed; we had no choice if we were going to live ourselves. Our march with the Partisans had taken us further east, and one morning they left us behind in a wood while they raided a village not far from the city of Varaždin. They returned with twenty prisoners, each one wired to the next. The Partisans had stripped the prisoners of their shoes and shirts, leaving them only their trousers, though the temperature could barely have been above zero. They were a miserable sight.

One of these prisoners, it transpired, was a brother of one of the Partisans, who, to demonstrate his loyalty to his mates, walked up to his brother, slapped him on the face and then jumped on his feet, probably breaking them. This happened right in front of us, in that camp in the woods. Eric seethed. 'He can't do that,' he growled at me. 'I'll have him.'

I clamped a hand over Eric's mouth and said, 'You'll keep out of it. This is political.'

When Eric visited me in Australia after the war, he said, 'I'm glad you jumped in when I was going to have a go at that bloke. They would have shot me for sure. You saved my life.' It was a lesson bitterly learned; you can't interfere in the politics of others — it's a game only the players understand.

The next night, near a village called Kalnik, a little to the south, not far from the Hungarian border, the prisoners were marched off into the dark. Next thing, I heard the unmistakeable report of artillery fire. I asked one of the Partisans what it was. 'Oh, that's the Hungarian border,' he said. But, of course, we never saw those poor prisoners again. Some time later on in our journey, a group of Partisans showed us two enemy prisoners they had locked up in a farmhouse. The men had been 'tried' and were to be shot that night.

While the Partisans were certainly brutal, and as careful as they could be to avoid casualties themselves, they were not invincible, either. Two members, a boy and a girl, had their legs blown off by a grenade while we were with the group, leaving them with only stumps. Their comrades put them in an old ammunition cart lined with straw, one at each end. It cannot have been comfortable. The bandages on their legs were clean, but the linen was rough. The paths were narrow and unsealed, and the cart had no springs and lurched all over the place. Those kids — they were just kids of maybe thirteen or fourteen — must have been in excruciating pain. Their faces were as pale as death. But they didn't say a word. We left them in a kind of bush hospital in Kalnik. I can't imagine that they survived.

16
GETTING OUT OF THE MADHOUSE

Our journey wound on through the mental asylum that was Croatia. In fact the route of the journey itself was pretty mental, for us. We zigzagged through the country. First east, then north-east, then south, and south-west, then east again. Some time in mid-May, in the middle of nowhere — I have no idea where we were — we were taken down a scrubby track to find a market that had seemingly sprung up out of the bush. It was only a small market, probably for local bartering, and the people trading were all elderly, but there in front of us were stalls with goods for sale! The wares looked and smelled mouthwatering: honeycomb oozing with the honey in it, barbecued goat and lamb, and hot bread. We were still in our British uniforms, which we'd patched and cleaned as best we could — if I do say so myself, we looked pretty good in battledress — and the stallholders pitched their wares to us frantically, probably thinking that we had money. We sure wished we had.

The Partisans, of course, had no uniform, apart from their caps. They wore whatever military clothing they could lay their hands on: German uniforms, British uniforms, the uniforms of local militia, clothes they made themselves and combinations of all of the above. We might have looked smart in our kit by comparison, but, oh, how I wished we'd had some money for some of that honeycomb. The Partisans never seemed to have any money. They lived mainly by the charity and goodwill of their supporters. It must have been part of their military strategy not to harass the people — for money or food, at least — and they didn't beg this day. I think they had taken us along to this little gathering just to show us that there were pockets of peace in their land, where old folk could get along with their business as they always had. Curious thing was, nearby this little market stood a machine gun — an enemy gun — festooned with colourful flowers. I'd never seen a gun with flowers on it before; these people were evidently proud of it.

Not far past this market, we ran into a British army soldier called Captain McKay — not a fellow POW on the run, but a liaison officer. He had been flown in to join the Partisans and act as a conduit of information between the

Allies and the resistance, and to report back on escaped POW numbers to co-ordinate repatriation missions. He couldn't do anything for us directly in this far-flung place, and the Partisans were clearly already looking after us, but he wished us well on our journey. He gave Allan a letter to give to his girlfriend, Lily, in Naples — which seemed an odd request at the time, since we had no idea if or when we'd ever get to Naples ourselves. Perhaps it was information he was passing on to a fellow agent that couldn't be despatched any other way; who would know? Allan would eventually deliver that letter and report back to me that if 'Lily' was an agent she was a rather voluptuous one.

To add to the general oddness of that day in Croatia, there were three mysterious people, two men and a woman, who'd been travelling along in the same direction as us, but were keeping apart from the Partisans. They also stopped to talk to McKay. The blokes were wearing broad-brimmed black hats, and all three wore long, drab gabardine coats, almost to the ground. After speaking briefly with McKay, they approached me and asked, if I got out, would I contact a friend of theirs in Palestine to let her know I'd seen them in Croatia. It seemed that they were German, or perhaps Austrian, Jewish refugees. They didn't tell me anything of their story, but perhaps their request was important, so I agreed. They then gave me an address in Tel Aviv, which I memorised rather than wrote down, because anything written down —

addresses, names, or diaries — could become incriminating in the wrong circumstances and I didn't know who these people were. Their friend's name, I remember well, was Ilse Stern. Only later, much later, back in Australia, did I twig to what might have been going on here, when Ilse Stern wrote back to me, asking me to come to Tel Aviv to talk about where I had seen her friends. That was a very weird request, to say the least, and putting two and two together, I think 'Ilse' mistakenly thought I was a Stern Gang sympathiser. I was certainly sympathetic to the plight of the hundreds of thousands of Jews displaced in Europe by the Nazis — that was one of the reasons I'd joined up in the first place — but not so to the Jewish underground militia that went about blowing up British peacekeepers and police in Palestine. I didn't write back to Ilse Stern, nor did she write to me again. That was a relief. Still, I've always wondered what happened to those three lonely travellers in that remote area of Croatia. I hope they made it out. The Partisans gave Jews and other civilian refugees safe passage, but no assistance as such, because there was nothing in it for them — unlike with us, who were basically being protected and assisted in exchange for arms. I hope the Ustashi didn't get them, or they, like so many millions of European Jews, would have been murdered.

We met another curious traveller on our journey around that time. In a village called Ravna Gora, towards the end of May 1944, we were told by one of the Partisans that

With a group of Partisans. I'm second from the right, looking surprisingly well presented in British battledress. The British liaison officer, Miss Lieutenant, is in the centre, Allan is on her right and Eric is behind him. An odd 'happy snap' amid the chaos of that time.

there was an Englishman in the area and we might like to have a chat with him, just to enjoy having a chat in our own language. Well, this 'him' turned out to be a girl, wearing a Royal Air Force uniform and toting a revolver on her hip. She was an interpreter, I think, also involved in helping arm the Partisans. Miss Lieutenant, we dubbed her, but we didn't chat for long: she was heading off to her mission headquarters somewhere or other — with that revolver on her hip. Not that women carrying arms was an unfamiliar sight to us now. The Partisans weren't at all sexist about the gender of their soldiers, and there was a strict rule of no hanky-panky in the ranks — not to protect the girls, but because a pregnant girl made a fairly poor soldier, and they needed every fighter they could get. There was none of this twenty-eight days behind bars for inappropriate liaisons, with the Partisans. Lay a hand on a girl and you'd be shot. At one point, one of us boys, I won't say which, might have been a bit sweet on one girl in particular, but you wouldn't risk death for a kiss, would you?

Our journey throughout that May remained haphazard, seemingly random to us. Slowly but surely, though, we were heading southwards, in the direction we needed to go, and as we went, we were swapped between small groups of Partisans, bands of usually about thirty or forty, and of many nationalities. The Partisans certainly were inclusive, of all who supported them militarily or politically. In the main they were

Slavs — Croats, Slovenians, Bosnians, Russians — but there were Austrians, Greeks, and a few Italians in the mix, too. Mostly, the grapevine worked to gain us acceptance into the next caravan, but every now and then, we were grilled about who we were and where we had been. Name? Rank? Battalion? By others — people devoted to their own cause and hugely appreciative of Allied assistance — we were treated like kings and given sincere handshakes. In one village we came to, the Partisans we were with seemed keen to show us that they weren't anti-capitalist, either. Capitalists, so long as they supported the cause, were okay, and to prove it they took us to visit a fairly well-to-do couple, where the lady of the house sat us down to a lovely meal of meat and potatoes. The couple spoke a few words of English, too, enough for us to make our hearty appreciation of their hospitality clear. It was a rare moment of almost civilised existence.

But as for the Partisans' actual cause, it all seemed Greek to me. As far as I could tell they wanted both communism and democracy, with a bit of capitalism on the side. Now, I didn't know as much about politics then as I do these days, but I still can't work that one out. Some of them were, in my opinion, just plain pigs. Of course, we were still on the run, and living rough and wild, sometimes in abject squalor, but one night, while trying to sleep in an old farmhouse full of lice, bugs and stinking, squawking chickens, we had to put up with a bunch of Partisans who got busy cooking themselves up some meat at midnight, walking all over us as they did so, not offering to share any of it with us — not that we expected them to — but splattering us with bits of sinew and gristle as they cooked and ate. I might have lost most of my own manners along the way too, but, politically or otherwise, I think that's simply called selfish and disgusting. Not that we could complain.

We'd learn quite a few political lessons with the Partisans, one of them on a night we stopped at an old castle. I don't know where we were, somewhere still up in the north of Croatia, but the castle was much like the one we had seen above the River Drava in Slovenia: a majestic, medieval fortress. It reminded me of the castles I'd read about in books on the Crusades: a place to make you wonder at all the history that'd gone on there. Of course, there's nothing so ancient in Australia, not of the Europeans at least, so I was pretty keen to have a look inside, and impressed that we'd be kipping in such a five-star establishment. The place was deserted, and we and several dozen Partisans entered via great stone steps, then went into a room with a massive hearth ten feet across: we'd be warm tonight. The walls were lined with paintings and bookshelves — still full — and sets of pistols and swords. But some of the paintings had been slashed, and the floor was littered with broken furniture and other debris. At the top of a staircase there was a suit of armour, complete with broadsword. One of the Partisans drew it and gave it to me.

I guess it was a kind of gesture of goodwill. But it weighed a ton and was four feet long. It would have been impossible to carry with us, though I wished we could have taken it. It was also weird to think you could steal such a thing, so I just tossed it in a corner somewhere. These Partisans we were with had no such moral concern, or appreciation of history: I watched as one of them picked up the sword and used it to slash a leather lounge and some more of the paintings round the place. The reason? These were symbols of capitalist greed. I might have been feral myself, and just a country boy from Drouin, but it looked like vandalism to me. And wasteful: why on earth would you wreck a twelve-foot-long lounge?

~

It was hard on the face of it to understand where that impulse for pointless destruction came from, but in the larger picture of Croatia it made some sort of sense. On occasions, as we travelled along roads in 'safe' Partisan territory, we'd see mile after mile of destruction. House after house after house had been burned down by the Ustashi. The reason? So the Partisans would find no comfort, no food and no cover in those areas. Scorched-earth tactics it's called, but you'd think, hundreds of families used to live in these houses; how are they ever going to rebuild?

Danger was never far away, and wherever we went Croatia remained a place of constant confusion. One village would belong to the Partisans, the next to enemy forces, and it was impossible for Eric, Allan and I to know which was which — half the time it seemed the Partisans themselves didn't know either. It put us constantly on edge. Periodically, our caravan would be halted and challenged by other Partisan patrols. It was always a nerve-racking experience. They had no way of knowing whether we were friend or foe until a few words were exchanged. It always put the wind up us. One night we were forced to scurry down the main street of a town controlled by the enemy. There we passed a house that was almost burned out, still smouldering. The Ustashi had been at work in the neighbourhood, trying to frighten residents from giving aid to the Partisans. Even with the adrenalin pumping, the charred house was a sobering sight, a symbol of the constant threat the people lived under: this town could be burned out entirely, coldly and mercilessly, if the Ustashi so chose.

Guerrilla wars such as that being waged by the Partisans have no front lines, and we were constantly on the move, avoiding open confrontation with the enemy — which explained why our route was so all over the place. Even when we were camped somewhere, we couldn't get too comfortable. Another night, the Partisans we were with were called to a meeting in a village about three or four miles away from where we were staying in the wilds. They invited us to come with them, and we accepted reluctantly, feeling obliged to tag along. We were tired and wanted to sleep. We rode in a wagon, with fixed seats, drawn by two horses; at least it made a change from walking. At length, we found an old stone building plastered with Partisan stars and flags. But when we went inside, we were told that the meeting had been cancelled because the enemy was only a couple of miles away. Nothing for it but to turn around and go back the way we came, and the three of us were relieved at that. The Partisans would not let us carry arms, remember, so we would have been helpless if we'd been attacked.

As we headed ever south, we had to keep to well-forested terrain and skirt the Croatian capital, Zagreb, which was, like all the bigger towns and cities, a Ustashi stronghold. Now, at this point we had to cross the Sava River in order to continue southward, but because the Ustashi held all the bridges and safe crossings in the area, we had to cross at what must have been the river's most treacherous stretch. Apparently, in Zagreb itself, the Sava is a pretty place for sightseeing, but as I looked at that water, I thought this was the fastest-flowing river I had ever seen. It wasn't a river; it was a black and swirling torrent coming off a roller-coaster. If you fell out of a boat into it, you would be swept away in seconds — no chance of surviving. Yet we had to cross the Sava to maintain our course, and cross we would, in a small wooden boat.

Getty Images 3242037

These are Partisans waiting to ambush a bridge. Surprise, brutality and the cover of dense forest were the key elements of their war.

The Partisans had rigged up ropes that passed between the two banks, a man on each side keeping them taut, and they were attached to the boat in order to hold our course steady. It all looked pretty flimsy and terrifying to me, and boy did it make for a hair-raising ride. For a start, when we loaded up the boat, two panicky Partisan girls stood up, causing the boat to rock precariously. Immediately, the air was thick with oaths and curses, telling them to sit down. They did, quickly. I'd discover later that a bunch of other POWs crossed in the same place but on the back of horses swimming furiously through the torrent — I suppose I should be grateful I wasn't with their party!

But there were moments of amazing beauty to be found within Croatia. As we soldiered on through the heart of the country, with every day that passed the land seemed to grow greener, with the bright deep summer greens of the new leaves opening out on the deciduous trees. It was mainly mountainous or hilly terrain we kept to, and to see great tracts of new life appearing all around us, to hear the woodpeckers peck-peck-pecking away in search of insects for their dinner, and to hear the song of the cuckoos whistling all day, well, it's a reminder that nature goes about her own business regardless of what us humans are up to. We've been here a long time, going about our business, too. I remember, in one village or other, peering down into an ancient communal well. It had seven perpendicular windlasses, and the sides were bricked with stone that looked as old as the hills, and were covered in moss. Leaning over the lip, you could just make out the water below. It must have been a hundred feet deep. I wondered what secrets it held.

There was never a lot of time for such contemplation, though. There can't be when your mind is in such a constant state of alertness, waiting, watching for what's going to come round the corner at you next. At one stage, we had to cross a railway line, knowing it was likely to be guarded. We set off in mid-afternoon, with several carts of ammunition, and by dark, we found ourselves in a small, hostile village, where we were told to be careful to keep our voices down, as enemy agents had been seen there not long previously. The Partisans sent out a patrol ahead of us to ascertain whether the railway line at this point was clear of Ustashi troops. Soon, they were back, talking excitedly: the advance party had climbed up the railway embankment, only for a hail of bullets to come whistling down the track. There were about thirty-five in our group at this time, too many to hope to get across the tracks safely. The Partisans decided to turn back. One of the horses pulling the carts was neighing like a steam train and we were sure before the night was finished we would 'get some lead', as they say. As it was, we were stopped by another Partisan patrol along the way — that was heart-stopping enough.

By the time we could get going again, it was late night, drizzling and so black that you couldn't see your hand in front of your face. We walked along a muddy track, slipping and sliding all over the place, and holding on to one another to make sure we stayed together. I was behind the leader, keeping a tight hold of him, when suddenly he tumbled into a big drain at the side of the track, probably eight foot deep. We had no warning and all toppled in on top of him. Among us at that time was an American aircraft crew who had been forced to bail out over Croatia and had now joined the Partisans. So there we all were in this dirty, deep ditch in the middle of nowhere, in the middle of the night — Yugoslavs, Australians, at least one New Zealander and these Americans — all of us swearing like blue murder, each in our own language. It must have made for quite a cacophony.

Eventually, we pulled ourselves out and made our way back to where we'd stayed the night before. It was not exactly palatial, just what we were used to: a shed full of chooks and pigs, foul-smelling and rotten with body lice. In such digs at night I made a point, wherever possible, of sleeping in a chair, facing backwards, head down on the backrest. That way, it took all night for the lice to climb up my legs. If you slept lying down on the floor, they were all over you in minutes. I cannot say loudly enough or often enough how much lice are not my favourite creature — from Italy to Austria to Slovenia to Croatia, they are all the same. Evil, excruciating, infuriating. They sow eggs in the hairs of your chest, and under your arms, everywhere there's hair, and when the young hatch, they give you hell. We were about to cop more of the human variety, though, the following night, when we went back to try to cross that railway line again.

This time on approach we got so close we all came under fire. You could hear the bullets whooshing through the air over us and past us, but couldn't see a thing, so we retreated back into the surrounding forest. Some time passed and there was much muttering and shouting. Then one of the Partisans said, 'Right, we'll cross the railway line now.' I think the leader of our group must have done a deal with the Ustashi guards, saying that we hadn't come to kill them, and would not attack them if they let us across. That is the only way to explain why we were being shot at one minute and crossing at our leisure the next.

But that wasn't quite the end of it. Allan, Eric and I were last across the track, along with two Yugoslavs. Suddenly, the two Yugoslavs were down on the track, working furiously to lay explosives. I know how to blow a railway line — we were taught that in commando school. It's not hard. You put a piece of TNT on each side of the rail, with a short length of instantaneous fuse between them. When they are set off together, the explosives split the rail clean in two, like a hot knife through butter. There is no way to repair it, except by laying a new rail.

So the Partisans blew up the railway line. This was war, after all. Of course, retaliation was instant and mortar and machine-gun fire crashed all around us. By this time we were in thick bush, and somehow I felt safe. It's so odd how your mind becomes hardened in war, even deluded; it's mystifying to me even today. I was thinking to myself, they'll shoot a lot of stray trees but won't get us. But when I think about it now, any one passing bullet could have been fatal — to me, Allan or Eric. I don't know what or who was looking after us, but we remained alive and intact.

Leaving the skulduggery behind at the railway line, we pushed on through the trees and found ourselves in a swamp. It was deep water up to my chest, so difficult for me, but impossible for one short young woman among the Partisans, who would have been in over her head. She was an Italian lass and had had a tough night, as we all had, but now she cracked up in tears. I was one of the tallest in our ragtag group and ended up piggybacking her through the night. It was slow and exhausting, one sloshing footstep after another, but what else could I do? I wasn't feeling particularly chivalrous at the time but I couldn't leave her there.

The leader of our group had a compass with him but I didn't have a lot of faith that he knew where he was going. We trudged through the swamp all night and when at last we emerged from it in the early hours of the morning, we were all virtual mudpacks, from head to toe. You would never have seen anything like it. Of course, we had nowhere to wash our clothes or ourselves. So we sat there, drying off in the sun. When we were ready, we dusted ourselves down and moved on.

Soon we arrived in an area which the Partisans must have had full control over — and they knew it. You could go for miles in any direction and not come across a Ustashi or German presence. In fact, we had not seen one German soldier after crossing the border into Croatia. I suppose the Partisans had harassed them with their guerrilla activity and the Germans had decided to leave the Ustashi to fend for themselves. The Germans couldn't have afforded to come to the aid of the Ustashi anyway, because by this time they constantly needed reinforcements on the Russian front, which had become their Achilles heel. The Germans never had enough soldiers to cover and hold the other areas they occupied, either: it was a recurring and ultimately fatal weakness. They had taken over nearly all of Europe, Norway and the Baltic states in the north, the Crimea in the south — and were now trying to hold on with threadbare forces.

It was around about this time that I struck up a friendship with one of the Partisans, a bloke called Puks Boris. He was twenty-one and had been a student at the University of Zagreb. He was a nice guy and we talked a lot about how the war was going and what might happen. He thought he might like to immigrate to Australia some day. One day, he gave me his Partisan cap as a gift. It is a distinctive cap, simple in design, like our AIF dress caps which we wore at a tilt on the head, but with a blazing red star at the front, and I treasured it. I still do. Later, Puks wrote to me in Australia — and his letters and that cap were to create extraordinary problems for me for a time back home.

For the time being, getting home, or at least getting out of Croatia, was more and more on my mind. We were heading towards Bosnia and I was feeling more and more confident about our chances of getting there. One morning the Partisans woke the three of us and said words to the effect of: 'You're coming for a feed.' They took us on a five-mile march into the hills, to a clearing where they had barbecued a pig. We ate heartily — fresh meat, newly baked bread and a sweet dessert wine that tasted glorious. The wine wasn't very alcoholic. In fact, the Partisans rarely drank, and I don't remember ever seeing one drunk. They liked to party, though. And after dinner there was a bit of a dance. And singing, of course. Life was almost good!

Nonetheless, to the last step this remained a country at war, with all its violence and privations bringing out the worst in people as well as the best. Mealtimes sometimes were as competitive and brutal as anything we had seen at the battlefront. On one occasion, as we neared the Bosnian border, Allan, Eric and I found ourselves alone with a big band of Partisans but no other Westerners. They were pretty primitive. One night they killed a pig and put it over a fire, not to scald the bristles off as we might have, but to burn the skin off altogether. Then they chopped it up with an axe and took the pieces to various houses in the neighbourhood for cooking. It wasn't a pretty sight, even for a butcher.

When the pig was ready for eating, we were taken to a small schoolroom crammed with about thirty desks and a blackboard. Politics now came into play. These Partisans were strict communists and didn't like capitalists such as us, who were also subjects of a king and queen. So we had to make do with a bit of pig's ear each, with lots of fat on it. It had been a while since we had eaten, and this gobful of hot, greasy food on an empty stomach acted like a packet of salts, threatening to go straight through me. But the Partisans' ideological mini-war was, like my stomach, only just getting started. Among them were three Russians, and as we ate, a voluble argument broke out between the Russians and the Yugoslavs. Suddenly, the Russians jumped up, slammed bullets into their rifles, covered the room and said something to the effect of: 'Anyone who moves is dead.' My first thought was to dive for the floor. If they opened up in that confined space there would be nowhere else to hide.

The argument, we soon learned, was over a little leftover pork. The Yugoslavs wanted to keep it for themselves, not throw it away on us dirty, rotten capitalists. The Russians argued that as communists, they were obliged to share what they had with everyone. Besides, they said, we were all on the same side, including us lousy capitalists, all in league against the fascists. They were sticking to the higher ideals of their politics — being very strict about their egalitarianism — and I admired them for it. After a while, everyone settled down again, and we all had a little more to eat.

The pork was good, almost as good as the thought that in just a little while longer, with any luck we had left over, we'd be out of this madhouse.

17
NO CONGRATULATIONS

We had been on the run for two months with the Partisans when finally in June we reached the outskirts of the city of Banja Luka, in the north of Bosnia. Many years later, in the 1990s, this city would feature tragically in the news during the years of 'ethnic cleansing' in Yugoslavia, but at this time, Banja Luka was our haven — we hoped. The area seemed free of any Ustashi presence — they'd obviously cleared out — and it was relatively safe for Allied planes to fly in here. The Partisans had cleared a patch of land for an airstrip — short, rough and sloping, but good enough. If all went well, Banja Luka would mark the end of our wanderings.

We made camp in the scrub outside the city, out by a railway line, surrounded by a few fields and fairly open country on the edge of a mountain valley basin and waited for about a week while the Partisans communicated with the Allies, who would then organise a plane to come in for us. During that time, we were joined by another US air crew who, like the other crew, had bailed out in Croatia. That made two American air crews in our midst. I don't know if they were a complete crew, or merely those who had survived; it was not the sort of question to ask. I do know that the two US crews loathed each other. One was a Liberator crew, the other a Fortress bomber crew, and they carried on like you'd wonder if they were fighting on the same side, with that stupid but entertaining competitiveness blokes from rival divisions, regiments or football teams can get caught up in. You would hear them all day calling each other 'Chicken shit!', 'C--- suckers!' One lot would say to us, 'Aw, don't talk to those chicken-shit c--- suckers,' et cetera, and the other would say the same, till after a while it wasn't very entertaining at all. To me, after what we'd come through, with the three of us having to stick by each other so closely, that type of juvenile spitefulness just seemed, well, juvenile; it'd be like me turning around and bagging Eric for being a Kiwi. Maybe it was the war, though, too. Someone's always fighting with someone, you've always got your back up, and for some blokes in some situations, any excuse to let off steam with abuse will do. For years I kept a US$1 bill with all their names on it, before I lost it, but they'll always be 'Chicken Shit' and 'C--- Sucker' to me.

Being Yanks and not POWs, they had a few of those dollars, and on occasion they used some to buy some cooked meat from the locals, which they shared with us. They were as generous as they could be; it wasn't much of a feed — you wouldn't call it a meal — but it was something. Every morsel helped. Set up where we were, not far from the middle of nowhere, there wasn't much in the way of food around. We couldn't just stroll off to Banja Luka to see if we could get a feed there. Even if we'd had money ourselves, we wouldn't have known what we'd find in town. Besides, we were on tenterhooks waiting for word about our plane.

Over the week we took every opportunity we could to wash and clean. One day we were bathing in the shallow river there, naked of course, and on the other bank there were women washing clothes, about fifty yards away. They didn't care: I'm sure the war had shown them worse. Our experiences had stripped us down, literally, to our basic humanness and it'd take us a while to recover the normal modesty of civilisation. I remember Allan laughing that each of us looked like a drover's dog. We were in fairly good nick, but skinny as rakes, stringy, all ribs and sinew, nothing to us except what hung off the bones. We were having a great old splash around in this cool, gentle water. It ran only about two or three feet deep, from an underground stream coming straight out of the side of a mountain, and there was a water wheel nearby, which the locals used to power a crusher for the grains that made their bread. It was an idyllic spot and we were happy in the moment, just being humans in our skins. Until one of the women yelled out to us across the water, gesturing to show that a snake was wiggling its way across. Soon we could see it, head up, making for us, all aggressive, like a tiger snake. We scrambled to the bank, looking for a stick to kill it, but couldn't find one. Eric, ever a forthright bloke, got hold of a wet shirt and hooked into it. The makeshift weapon worked: he killed the snake. We spent the rest of that afternoon sunbathing and picking lice from our skin and hair and burning them from the seams of our clothes with hot coals, getting rid of as many as we could, and I had to pause to reflect upon what a shame it would have been for one of us to have got done in by snakebite after all we'd been through to get this far.

On June 10 — more than two months since we had broken out of the prison camp in Austria — we were told that a plane was coming in at 9.45 that night. We could hardly contain our excitement. The Partisans had built up little piles of wood along the edges of the runway and lit them to act as flares lighting the path. Duly, we heard the plane on its approach at 9.45. But the night was foggy, and despite the help of the fires, the plane overshot the runway. We watched helplessly as it disappeared down the side of a hill!

Desperately, we ran after it and found it about a quarter of a mile away, bogged in a swamp, barely six foot short of a railway embankment. It was an incredible stroke of luck that none of the crew on board was hurt. The swamp had given them a soft, smooth landing, but that embankment … if they'd hit that at speed, it would have been the end of them.

As it was, the captain jumped out to greet us and surveyed the plane. 'Well, guys,' he drawled, as only a Yank can, 'I guess we'll have to burn it.'

This was, of course, fairly standard practice in the event of a crash, so that the enemy couldn't get their hands on the aircraft. But that night there were two Australians and one New Zealander who weren't going to have any of that. 'Don't you bloody dare,' we yelled. 'We can see the wheels. We can get it out.' In fact, we threatened to kill the captain if he burnt the damn plane. So he let us see what we could do.

We pitched in to cut down saplings to camouflage the plane for when daylight came and enemy spotter planes might make a nuisance of themselves. The next morning, we set to work, digging channels into the mud and slush, and lining them with slats of wood that some locals brought to us from nowhere. Like magic they arrived with these slats, about the thickness of a brick, perfect for laying tracks for the plane's wheels, and we laid them in a feathered pattern, like strips of parquetry flooring. It was quite a feat of impromptu and communal makeshift engineering. As we beavered away, the Yanks said to us in their usual laconic drawl, 'Reckon you boys'll get a medal from the President for stopping us from burning the plane.' We just laughed that off. Their appreciation was nice, but we weren't after an award for our efforts — we simply didn't want to have to wait for another plane. To have burned it, when there was an alternative, would have seemed an extraordinary waste to us. We got a reward anyway, for our troubles. In the plane's emergency supplies was a gallon tin of peanut butter. It was irresistible. We dragged it to a strategic spot, cut the lid off and put a stick in it, then every time we walked past we had a mouthful to cheer us on with our digging. By geez, it was good! I can't tell you how wonderful that peanut butter tasted. By the time we had laid those tracks for the plane, we'd finished the whole tin — the bottom of it was shiny.

By 4 p.m., we were ready for the plane to be hauled out of the swamp. But how? This wasn't exactly a tiny aircraft: it was a ten-ton DC-3. But as if by magic again, forty bullocks turned up from somewhere and were hitched up to the plane in a line of twenty pairs yoked together. The locals called out whatever their word is for 'giddy-up', and at first, nothing much happened. The problem was that there were too many bullocks to co-ordinate. By the time the last few were ready to go, the first few had stopped. So they cut the numbers back to ten pairs and before you knew it, they had dragged that old plane out of the mud and back along the runway to where we had been waiting the previous night — about a quarter of a mile up the hill.

Once on the airstrip, the Americans tested the hydraulics. Without them, we might have been able to take off but we wouldn't have been able to land. Blessedly, they were still in good working condition. We were a multicultural lot that boarded — thirty-one of us in all on that plane. Apart from ourselves there were a couple of Frenchmen, some Czechs, the American air crews and an English navigator. Most American planes flying into Yugoslavia had English navigators. This was because the English underwent more thorough training, passing through four stages to the Americans' three, and were more scientific in their approach to map references and co-ordinates. It was an important skill in an area where precision mattered. The Yanks' way, more often than not, was to blow the top off a hill and say they'd fixed Berlin!

The first thing I did as we were getting on the plane was to give my boots away to one of the locals, swapping them for a pair of rope sandals. I figured that where I was going, there would be plenty of boots. I had been wearing my boots for so long I hadn't realised that in one of them, a nail had been driving up through the remains of the lining into my foot, causing a papilloma, a gristly wart-type thing, like a corn. I didn't feel it because it had happened slowly, and I had adapted. But the bloke who got my boots would have felt it!

On board, the crew were apprehensive. They did not know if they could clear a range of hills about two miles away. So they got all the Partisans on the ground to hold onto a part of the plane: tail, strut, wing, undercarriage, whatever. Then they revved the engines so hard I reckon all the rivets popped out. Finally, someone yelled out in the local lingo: 'Let her go!' The plane shot down the airstrip as if jet propelled. Within minutes we had risen over the mountain range and turned towards the coast. Allan, Eric and I were too tired and relieved to appreciate it too much at the time, but it was really quite a moment. Against the odds, we had made good our escape.

~

We landed in Bari on Italy's Adriatic coast at about 2 a.m. the next morning, June 12. This, by now, was friendly territory. Allied forces had long since been up that side of the country and reclaimed it. At the airfield, we were met by vehicles from an English regiment and taken to their base camp. There was a guard on the gate, who gave us some cigarettes and showed us to a tent. Another soldier threw us a blanket — one between the three of us — and we lay down on the ground inside the tent and immediately fell into a deep and blissful sleep. It was hardly a heroes' welcome, but in the context of war, we were not heroes, merely soldiers who had been good at their job and lucky enough to make it back.

We didn't celebrate among ourselves, not even with a handshake. We just thought it was bloody good to be somewhere safe again, with the prospect of a decent feed.

That was celebration enough. As well, we'd been told the latest about the war: the Allied invasion of Normandy had begun on June 6, D-Day, the second front was opening up against the Germans, which meant they'd now have to fight the Allies in the north-west, and the Russians in the east, all on European soil, and that was exciting news. It felt like, not only were we safe, but the Allies were closing in — they were going to win this damn thing.

We woke at daybreak and went to find something to eat. In the mess, where the Brits had already had their breakfast, a loaf of white bread was sitting on a table. There was nothing else, no butter, no spread, just a humble loaf of plain white bread. We didn't care. We tore into it with our hands and gulped it down as if it were a feast. We were like kids at a party when the sponge cake comes out.

Outside the door there was a hot copper, where the soldiers washed their dixies after eating. Eric asked the bloke working around there if we could have some of the hot water for a wash. 'Piss off,' came the reply. See what I mean about a heroes' welcome! Eric, fiery as ever, grabbed him by the throat, forced him against the copper and said: 'We're having some of that hot water if I've got to kill you to get it.'

Eric couldn't abide injustice, in even the smallest form. He would spark up at the mere scent of it. Some nob came along and asked what was happening. Eric said, 'We've been over in bloody Yugoslavia. We haven't had a proper wash for months. We're covered in dirt, lice, our clothes stink. All we want is some hot water.' The nob understood. 'Give 'em all the hot water they want,' he said.

We got new uniforms, too, and a better tent, outside the camp. 'Do as you please,' they told us. 'Anything you want, just come in and get it.' So we did. Bread, tinned herrings ... it doesn't sound like much, but to us, these were luxuries.

That first day, Allan and Eric went out to have a look at the shops in Bari, a civilising experience. They came back and told me they'd had a couple of beers and thoroughly enjoyed themselves. I couldn't go with them because I still had no boots, just the stinking pair of rope slippers I'd swapped for my boots in Yugoslavia. They wouldn't have gotten me as far as the front gate of the camp!

~

After a few days, we made our way from Bari via Taranto to Naples for a debriefing. Part of the journey was with an American who picked us up in a Jeep. He was a lunatic who drove with his foot flat to the floor the whole way, even though we were mostly on winding country roads. Around one corner we came upon an Italian farmer on a horse-drawn cart, carrying a huge barrel. It was impossible for him to get off the road; it was just too narrow. But rather than wait, the Yank tooted and bulldozed the cart, tipping it over and smashing the barrel. He must have injured the farmer, too, or killed him for all I know. The Yank didn't stop; he just yelled, 'Don't you know there's a war on!' His attitude was typical of too many I saw who seemed to think that war gave them a licence to do as they please. He simply didn't give a stuff.

In Naples, the British army debriefing officer questioned us at length about where we'd been and what we'd seen, and was pleased to hear from us that there appeared to be no Germans left in the areas of the Balkans we'd travelled through, and no strong Ustashi presence in the south of Croatia and north of Bosnia. He looked the three of us up and down and asked, 'Now, do any of you want to go back to Yugoslavia?' I was the only one who said yes. I don't know why I did. I wasn't afraid to go back, or to do whatever I was told to, but I can't have been thinking very straight. Allan and Eric just looked at me as if to say, 'You bloody idiot.' I don't know what the officer made of me; he just nodded, 'Right.' I'm sure he appreciated my willingness, but he probably realised I wasn't quite with it, because he didn't take me up on it, didn't mention it again, and I didn't get called to go back — thank heavens.

While we were in Naples, we also learned that the Allies had finally captured Rome from the Germans, just the week before. Someone asked if I would like to go to see the famous city while I was on leave. I replied, 'What the hell for? It's just some old buildings.' I felt the same about Naples. 'See Naples and die,' the saying goes, meaning the place is so beautiful you'll be overwhelmed. That's about right, too. I was overwhelmed — by the dirty, narrow, little streets, and washing hanging out windows everywhere. People still say to me, 'Why don't you go and have a look at Europe?' I always answer, 'What the hell for? It's just the same as here: rivers, grass, trees, people.' I've got no inclination to go back. People forget that I saw a bit more of Europe close up than I ever wanted to in 1943 and 1944.

No, I was going home. The three of us went back to Bari to await our orders and transport, and there we saw a sight. A bunch of Maori infantry had just arrived, fresh from capturing Rome, battle-fatigued and armed with gallon tins full of red wine. They were a fun crowd of blokes, and amazing soldiers, but we only had a couple of drinks with them and left before the inevitable brawl erupted. Allan and I parted ways with Eric there, who rejoined his Kiwi comrades. There were no tears as we went our different ways. This was a time when public displays of emotion were not commonplace, and certainly not among blokes. We just said, 'See you later.' Besides, I don't think we fully grasped yet what we had achieved, or that it was really all over. Of course, I had no idea that it would be forty-six years before I saw Eric again.

Allan and I went by boat to Alexandria. On board we met up with some Australians who had also been with the

Partisans in Yugoslavia — Harry Lesar and Ross Sayers. They'd ended up there after jumping a prison train from Greece in 1941 and initially had linked up with Michailovic's rebels before sniffing the wind and joining Tito. Harry, whom I had met way back at training camp at Balcombe when I joined up, had, after three years of rambling through Yugoslavia, learned the local lingos and had made himself useful as an interpreter. He was a man with a reckless streak, too. At Alexandria, he said he wanted to get off the ship to have a look around. When I said that he had to have a leave pass, he replied: 'You can stick your leave pass. We're getting off the boat.'

So we took off down the gangplank. At the first fish-and-chip shop we found, we ordered steak, chips, tomatoes and three eggs each. When we were finished, we looked at one another and said, 'What do you reckon, another one?' So we went again: steak, chips, tomatoes, eggs. And then we had a third helping! We had a few years to catch up on. Perhaps the authorities knew that, too — we didn't get into any trouble for it.

From Alexandria, we went by train to the outskirts of Cairo, near the Pyramids at Giza, where the army had a camp. Soon as I set foot in the place, I developed a fearful cold. I'd spent months walking through rain and sleet and slush, sleeping on the frozen ground, waking up so cold I was shaking and couldn't talk, but never got a cold. Now I could hardly talk! It must have been that, once my mind knew I was out of danger and relaxed, so did my immune system.

Still, I might not have been able to talk but I could write. Not only did I send that letter off to 'Ilse Stern' but by this time we'd got word of Eric and what I heard gave me reason to write fairly urgently. We'd heard that Eric had been arrested by the military police in Cairo. There'd been some sort of disturbance in an army comfort house in which he was staying, and the military police had turned up to arrest some bloke. Eric, in just his shirt-tails, climbed out of bed, demanding to know what was going on. So he was arrested, too, and taken to the Cairo military jail. I was furious at this news. I wrote a letter to the governor of the jail saying Eric should be regarded as a hero, not a thug. I wrote about his courage on the riverbank that awful, endless night in Austria. 'You wouldn't get a braver act in your life,' I said, and outlined why he deserved a VC rather than a prison sentence. My letter was passed on to the military authorities, and it was this same letter that would have, if it hadn't been for my lowly NCO status, seen Eric get a VC. I was pretty passionate about it, you could say. Not that I'd find this out for many, many years, but at the time Eric was sitting having a cup of tea with the governor of the jail, who, it turned out, was the brother of someone Eric knew. Kiwis! They all know each other.

Anyway, we laid up for a week in Cairo, not up to much, then we were taken to the Suez Canal and loaded onto a freighter. At the end of the canal, we joined a huge convoy of about forty ships heading for Bombay to deliver supplies bound for General Mountbatten in Burma. There were many West Africans on the ships, recruited to act as carriers in the Asian jungle. Allied command figured that they could handle the heat. They were on deck every morning, in spanking new uniforms, drilling. They loved it — so much you'd think the worst punishment for an African would be to bar him from the parade ground.

We stayed in Bombay for a week. Harry Lesar and I cleared off the boat again, and we went to visit a family he knew there, a lady whose husband was fighting in Burma and her daughter. It was lovely to sit there and have a meal with them, but it also made me realise just how much I'd changed. I felt awkward in their company, in their nice house, and shy, like I must have stunk or something. I didn't, of course, but after so long knowing I did stink, I suppose it felt odd not to. At one point I got worried that the boat would leave without us, but Harry was blithe. 'Nah, it won't go without us,' he said. I remember looking at him and thinking, you're a wild man, too. We both were — looking smart in our uniforms on the outside but still pretty wild on the inside.

Eventually, they put us on another freighter. For the first day out of Bombay, we had a warship as an escort but by the next morning it was gone. We didn't see another boat, nor land, for the next six weeks, a very long trip. Our freighter, all alone as it was, was forced to keep out of shipping lanes and avoid getting too close to the north-western coast of

The wild men return. From left to right: Ross Sayers, me, Allan Berry and Harry Lesar — at Port Melbourne, September 11, 1944.

Australia, so as not to run into any Japanese warships. We headed due south — we knew that because it got progressively colder by the day — and all we had to do was play cards and sing songs: 'You Are My Sunshine', 'The Last Time I Saw Paris'. They were not new, but they were to us; our lives had been on war-hold for four years. We thought these songs were great; they reminded us of our freedom. Harry had got his hands on a gramophone, so we sat on the deck all day, playing records and bridge.

The next land we saw was Point Lonsdale, near the entrance to Port Phillip Bay, on September 11, 1944. I had begun to think I would never see Australia again. I'd begun to feel that I was just a wild animal, roaming the world, without a home. Now we were steaming up the bay on a Saturday afternoon, listening to a football match between Carlton and South Melbourne on the radio, and I remember thinking, geez, this is good.

Mum and Dad were waiting on the wharf for me, which was wonderful. They had had only sparse news of me in the time I was away. They found out that I had been wounded at Tobruk by reading the newspaper, and again when I was taken prisoner at El Alamein. Official confirmation from the Red Cross would have come much later. My sister Nancy was working in the intelligence section of the army at Prahran, so she quickly knew that I had escaped the POW camp. But she could not have known that I was safe behind enemy lines; no-one did. I would have been listed as 'Missing from camp, presumed escaped'. The next they would have heard was after the debriefing at Bari. It must have been a rotten time for them, not knowing and fearing the worst all that time. But now I was back where I belonged. I hugged my parents, and I kissed my mum. I didn't cry — but I did want to kiss the ground as well. It was four years, less four days, since I'd left.

Home sweet home. Mum and Dad were pretty happy to see me, and I them, needless to say. The little fellow in Mum's arms is my new nephew, my brother Alex's baby son, Robert Ernest Brough — oblivious to it all.

18
WILD MAN RETURNS

At the dock, Allan and I were interviewed and photographed for the *Sun News-Pictorial.* Then that night, Allan left for the three-day train trip back to Perth, and I caught a train home to Drouin with Mum and Dad. It was so good just to be sitting on that train with them; and funny, too. I was that excited I kept letting the swearwords slip out as I spoke — in front of my mum! She pretended she didn't notice. I think she'd worked it out. I'd spent all that time in the world of blokes, day in, day out, where every second word was 'f--k' or variations thereof. I couldn't help it. I'd have to retrain my mouth.

The story of our escape and return had appeared in the Melbourne *Herald* on the morning of our arrival, and had gone

Me and my sister Marjorie in Drouin, 1944. She married a fellow called Noel Harrison, of the 7th Division, while I was away.

on ahead of me to Drouin. At the station there were about five hundred people waiting to welcome me, and a banner saying something about the return of the little hero. It was a bit overwhelming; a lot overwhelming, actually, considering I hadn't acknowledged to myself what I'd done yet. I didn't feel like a hero, so why would I expect to be treated like one?

On the platform, two blokes I knew were waiting to get on the Melbourne train. I'd have preferred to talk to them but I didn't get a chance. One was Len Dingwall, who was in my class at school. I'd find out later that he had won a Distinguished Conduct Medal at El Alamein when he took out three machine-gun posts on the one raid, on the very same night I was taken prisoner. You'd never guess it: he was

such a quiet, modest man. He was a sergeant who had become
a lieutenant, and now was heading back to the Pacific Islands.
He was wearing his brand-new pips as he was getting on the
train, but I couldn't get to him to chat because the crowd was
mobbing me. Couldn't do anything but nod and wave.

The other guy was Ted Gould, who still lives in Drouin
as I write. I'd find out later that he had been a coast watcher
in New Guinea, hiding out in the hills with the natives and
reporting on Japanese shipping movements. Periodically, one
of the natives would tell the Japanese that there was a 'white
man with machinery' up there, so he had to keep on the move

Back in civvies.

every two or three days. Len was heading back to the islands this day, too.

The next few weeks were a bit crazy. My old boss, Mr Winters, good as his word, had held a job for me at the butcher's, and Mum and Dad had moved down from Myrtleford so that Dad could help out at the shop to make certain of it. In fact, Mr Winters was ready for retirement and said I should go into partnership on the place with his old assistant. But I was still in the army. I wouldn't be returning to civilian work for a while to come yet. There was a war still on.

First, though, I had six weeks of leave, and during that time in Drouin, a letter arrived informing me that I had won the Military Medal. The citation praised my 'courage in persistent attempts to escape POW camps'. I don't know who nominated me, but I presume it was the debriefing officer at Naples. Most escapees were decorated in some way. The first person I thought of was my mother. I hadn't treated her very well when I left. I hadn't given enough consideration to the wrench it must have been for her. '*See you later,*' I'd said to her as she cried, and I'd gone off to war with that silly dream in my head: I was going to bring her home a VC, just like Albert Jacka, I was going to make her proud. But when the bullets started flying, I abandoned all thoughts of medals and honouring my mum. I thought only of survival. Now, not only was I back, but with a medal, and Mum could be proud.

Actually, I didn't get the medal immediately. I was presented with it at a ceremony at Government House in Melbourne in 1946, by the chief justice, Sir Edmund Herring. Mum came with me to the presentation, and I'm sure she shed a tear. In the meantime I was allowed to wear a ribbon on my chest, denoting where the medal one day would hang.

Still, while I looked all right on the outside, the perfect model of a returned soldier, I wasn't *all* all right. Maybe it was the confusion of being back in a world that should have been familiar but had become strange to me, but I got this dreadful shake in my left hand. I suppose it was some shell-shock type of thing — occasionally I still get a little tremor in it today — but at the time I really didn't know what it was, and it was a lot more pronounced. It was so bad that if one of the nice older ladies I knew in town invited me round for a cup of tea with the Country Women's Association, I'd make up an excuse not to go. I'd say, 'Oh, thanks, but I might be a bit busy this afternoon,' or something. I was embarrassed about the shake. With my left hand, I literally couldn't have held a cup of tea steady — I'd lose half of it in my lap. I was also still not really with it. I'd take off to Melbourne, without a word to Mum; I'd just take off. She'd go up to the station to ask the stationmaster if he'd seen me. Invariably he'd say, 'Yes, Mrs Brough. I saw Ernie get on the Melbourne train this morning.' I needed to be with my mates; well, not even mates

— just anyone from the army, from my world. I'd disappear into it, sometimes for days at a time.

During this time I received the standard medical checks from the army. I was sent with others to the Heidelberg Repatriation Hospital in Melbourne's northern suburbs and spent two weeks there. We had blood tests and who knows what other tests. They were watching to see how mad we were. I must have passed: they didn't want to keep me there. One of the nurses seemed more interested in hitching herself up to a solider — any of us. I wasn't interested in anything like that. Well, there was one nurse there I might have taken a shine to. Shirley, her name was, but she was Jack Walsh's sweetheart — my old mate Jack's girl — and he hadn't yet come home. He'd marry her when he did.

For about a month after the check-up, a few of us returned soldiers were sent out to work selling war bonds in Melbourne. Obviously, they figured that it would be hard for people to refuse uniformed soldiers, freshly back from war. The sympathy vote would be big. I had a great time doing that, mostly selling to the owners of factories and businesses. One day I would be at a wool-scouring plant in Footscray, the next at Ossie Porter's shoe factory in Clifton Hill. Porter was a well-known racehorse owner of the time and a very generous, community-minded bloke. When we turned up he and his staff sang 'The Brown Slouch Hat' to us. I sold him and others lots of bonds. As most who know me would tell you, I can string a few words together when it's needed. The idea was we'd tell people what it was like on the front — the conditions, the danger — to pull the heartstrings and open the purse strings. I remember, after one of my chats on a floor at the Taxation Office, one woman came up to me and told me I should write a book — well, there would be a 64-year wait for that, wouldn't there! There was no such thing on my mind then. I was just happy to be doing something.

The bloke we were working for was a civil servant of some kind, Bill Patten was his name, and we became quite good friends. He said I should apply for a full-time job selling bonds when I got out of the army. But I wasn't interested enough to make a career out of it. In any case I figured there wouldn't be much call for war bonds once the thing was over, and I couldn't see myself as a civil servant, pushing a pen behind a desk.

From Melbourne I was then sent off to an army camp at Ballarat, to be rehabilitated back into army life proper. When I got there, though, I had a more urgent problem to deal with. Suddenly, that papilloma corn in my foot felt like a fat piece of glass — after all the time I'd been walking around on it, it only got sore now, as summer started coming on — and I had to have it cut out. As for the rehabilitation side of things, for the next six weeks I was put to work — this time making leather handbags. This might sound strange, but as always there was method in this military madness. I made these bags from scratch, and completely by hand. I'd cut and wet the leather,

This is one of a couple of newspaper shots taken of me in Drouin after returning. Lots of us returned 'heroes' were snapped liked this for all sorts of publications, to encourage the war effort. I didn't look too bad, did I? But on the inside I was still a bit wild.

make designs of roses and daisies, and groove them into the hide, then sew the pieces together — fully lined and with internal pockets, of course. I designed one that was a perfect circle, like a flat hatbox. It was red, and the zipper went the whole way round. Bag-making was finicky and painstaking work, but it helped me to get back into a routine. In a way it was no different from making that suitcase from those tins, back in PG57 — a sanity saver, which helped settle the shakes in my left hand a bit, too. And it gave me ready-made gifts for all my girlfriends. No, I'm not serious there! I did meet some nice girls in Ballarat, but at that time, I didn't think anyone would want to be my girlfriend.

Rehab was important. While I did leatherwork, others did carpentry. After the insanity of war and life on the run, it gave us a bit of time to sit and think about what had gone on in our lives. Some didn't cope with the return to 'real' life at all. I know of at least one bloke, the brother of a close mate, who suicided as soon as he got home, and the only reason why I won't name him here is because it was such a deep tragedy for his family. The stigma and shame of a suicide in those days was just dreadful. I'm sure there were thousands who took that road. But for someone like me, rehab did do its job; just to be making something with my hands again had a curing effect. But it would take a long, long time yet to work the war out of my system, to the extent that I could make my own peace with it.

Looking back now, I know I needed that handbag therapy, to tame the wildness that had grown inside me. Really, Allan, Eric and I had lived like dogs. Every day had been a dangerous day, every shadow a possible predator. We survived on instinct, so it was always going to be difficult to slip back into the civilised world. You would only have to look at me the wrong way back then and I'd have a go at you.

My behaviour on the train to Ballarat was a case in point. The carriage was full of soldiers, and I had had a few beers and was sitting on the floor having a smoke. Sitting on the floor didn't worry me: I'd been sitting on the bloody ground for years. Suddenly, a bloke said to me: 'Got a cigarette, Dig?'

I had an old tobacco tin, with no more than a bit of dust in it. I showed it to him and said, 'There you go, that's all I've got left, and I want to keep a fag for the morning.'

He was miffed. 'Oh, you rotten mongrel, you wouldn't give a bloke a smoke.' That didn't worry me much either, but a little while later, he reached into his pocket and pulled out a packet of cigarettes. Something inside me snapped. There I'd been a few years before, in a train carriage in Italy, a POW sharing one orange between eleven men. Now, in another crowded train, this bloke had had a go at me for not giving him my last bit of tobacco — and he had had a full packet of his own. I leaped off the floor and in two seconds had him by the throat. I was choking him and I meant to kill him. It took

Me on the left and Bert Cocks, back home, 1944.

three or four men to pull me off him. There was a part of me that was a bit insane, I suppose.

I'd also started drinking heavily. When I first arrived home, I had about £300 in my paybook. That would be something like $20,000 today. My dad asked me what I was going to do with it. I said, 'Spend it.' Just like that. He said I'd be sorry, but my mother said, 'Let him spend it.' I think she understood that I needed a way to let off a bit of steam, just as she understood what I got up to when I'd 'disappear' off to Melbourne. I'd grog on. I went everywhere I could, didn't spare a penny. I was off my face a lot of the time. Many days, come dinner time, I couldn't remember where I was, then couldn't remember where I'd had dinner. My mates would tell me, but it wouldn't ring a bell. It was a kind of desperation. But I think it saved me in a way, too. As I said, I'd been living like a wild man for months, and you can't just get that out of your system overnight. Nowadays, there would be all manner of counselling. Then, there was alcohol — and the rehabilitation camp at Ballarat.

My time in Ballarat was highly social, and that was important, too — having plain fun. My mates and I were out drinking and dancing nearly every night. In fact, we'd start drinking at our 10 a.m. break from rehab most days, popping out for a Ballarat Bertie for morning tea. Some of our adventures were epics. One night we had what we called a nine-gallon barrel dance. Another bloke and I carted a nine-gallon barrel of beer from Craig's Hotel near the Eastern Oval to a nearby hall, put a pump in and, music blaring, invited everyone in. We had a great night, drank till we passed out, but when we woke up at about 2 a.m., everyone was gone — and so was the barrel and the pump. This was alarming, since the pub was expecting its barrel back. We huddled around to make a plan. Near dawn, we found the blokes who had smuggled the barrel out, and brought it back to camp, narrowly saving our bacon. One of my collaborators was a bloke called Don Funston, a fellow wild man, who had tried to play dead to avoid being captured by the Germans — until one of them jabbed him in the arse with a bayonet. He had come through Yugoslavia with the Partisans, too — in fact, he'd been with that mob who crossed the Sava River on horseback. Don would later become my best man.

It was on one of our big nights out in Ballarat, in the same hall, that I met the girl who would become my wife, Edna May Stevenson. Fortunately, or magically, I wasn't pissed that night. And I couldn't have missed her. It was, corny as you like, love at first sight for me. She had doll's eyes, beautiful big green eyes, and she could dance. Boy, could she dance. What a stunner. She'd learned to jitterbug — a dance craze set off by the Yanks when they'd arrived in Australia earlier in the war — and she taught me to dance. Not the jitterbug, of course — Bandy Brough was ever a clod-foot who'd never go beyond a decent foxtrot — but with her in my arms, well, she made me feel light, from the moment of that very first dance. That night, I walked her back to her parents' place and sat outside against the fence, talking to her for hours, about anything and everything. Her parents lived in an old house. They were not wealthy people, but they lived in the street immediately across the road from the Eastern Oval, and her father had built a stile in the front yard so that he could see over the fence into the ground — there was an extra attraction for me! Finally, I had to go. We couldn't sit out there all night. I gave her a quick kiss, blink and you'd miss it, but that was it for me: I was stuck on a girl called Edna May.

Over the next couple of months, Edna May and I became quite pally — in other words, I didn't leave her alone. She worked at Morley's clothing mill, as a cutter, cutting out patterns. She had a pair of scissors that must have been a foot long, which she used for work, and she always kept them handy, just to keep me in order. It worked! One day we were at her place, talking as usual — I was always hanging about there — when her sister Hazel interrupted. 'You two are mucking around,' she said. 'Why don't you just get married and be done with it?' I couldn't have agreed more and, miraculously, Edna May felt the same way. We'd been an item for probably two months. I didn't want to wait any longer. Edna May's parents were all for it, too. I didn't even really ask her father, because for him it was a foregone conclusion. We got on well, he loved talking about the land — farming and the bush — and so did

I. Edna May's mum would affectionately say to me, 'Oh, you're nothing but a hopeless bushy.' They were pleased their daughter would marry. Problem was I was about to be posted to another base, in Singleton, miles away in New South Wales, and didn't have time to look around for engagement rings. So I gave Edna May £45 — quite a decent whack of money — and told her to buy one for herself. It wasn't very romantic, I'll admit, but I was still a serving soldier.

After three or four months in Ballarat, my mates and I were considered to be rehabilitated and fit for duty, and were sent off to Singleton. We thought we would be going back to our own units, but we weren't, and the redeployment proved to be a waste of time. For the next three weeks, we were sent out on manoeuvres, in the charge of a corporal. He took us on long route marches and tried to teach us to throw smoke bombs, but we would put them down rabbit burrows, chasing out the rabbits. After all we'd seen and done, route marches and smoke bombs seemed trivial and pointless. The exercises were just a way of keeping us out of the pub, I think. The corporal had never seen action and it was impossible for us to respect him. We didn't even call him corporal. 'Just wait until you get to the front line,' we'd say. 'You'll see what it's all about then.'

This was early June 1945. The Germans had surrendered in May, an event we didn't really celebrate, as we'd been expecting it. What we were all waiting for was for the Japanese to give up in the Pacific — it was obvious that their time was coming to an end, but they were hanging on. One day at Singleton they lined up eighty-three of us and said, 'Anyone with more than five years' service can apply for a discharge.' They told me that if I stayed on, I'd go straight to officers' school. Remember, I had been bound for officers' school in 1942 until I was taken prisoner at El Alamein. Army command knew this, and knew also that I had since won a Military Medal. If I'd stayed in the army then, I would have had a career as a permanent soldier. I would have gone to Korea, to Malaya, probably finished up in Vietnam as a lieutenant colonel. That is, if I was still alive. If the bullets had kept going past me. If my luck had held …

But I'd had enough. I'd been in the army for more than five years — at war or in a prison camp or on the run for four of them. I'd had some hellish times but some great times, too. I'd made many great mates and they stayed mates. But I'd also lost many. I was twenty-five; it was time to move on. Of the eighty-three in the line-up that day at Singleton, only three stepped forward to say they would stay on.

~

Edna May and I got married on August 4, in the Church of England in Ballarat. Our families were there with us and it was a lovely day; another proud day for my mum, too. She loved Edna May and it was a joy for her to see me settling

Our wedding day. Me, my lovely Edna May, her sister Phyllis, and my best man Don Funston.

down at last. As the atomic bombs dropped on Nagasaki and Hiroshima, my new wife and I were honeymooning in the Dandenong Ranges, in a place called Olinda. It was a pretty flash guesthouse, catering especially for lovebirds — perfect — although our married life got off to a shaky start. Noticing that there were plenty of rabbits about, I set some traps and got up early on the first morning to clear them. I came home with a couple of rabbits. 'This is terrible,' protested my wife. 'It's the first morning of our honeymoon and you're out catching rabbits!' Well, a country boy is always a country boy. Her mum was right — hopeless bushy.

It was only a week's honeymoon, and Japan surrendered soon after our return. The celebrations for this occasion were mammoth. Edna May and I tried to get into the centre of Melbourne that night to join in, but you couldn't move for all the people.

Melbourne would be our home, though. Our first home was a room in a boarding house in the suburb of Northcote. I'd taken a job at a butcher's shop in Bourke Street in the heart of the city, just for a fresh start, something different from the country life I'd led. The shop was called Watkins, and its main business was sausages; they made tons of them, and sold them to cafes and restaurants. It bugged me, though, that they never seemed to clean the shop or anything in it. It ran against the grain of what I'd learned about good butchering. So I would go back after dinner and rake up the filth beneath the machines. This turned out to be a bad move. The union blokes got onto me and asked me why I was working during my dinner hour. Watkins, the boss, called me into his office. He was quite a nice bloke, but pretty obviously he didn't want trouble. He also asked me why I was flouting union rules and working in my dinner hour. When I tried to explain, he asked if I wanted to leave. I replied, 'Well, if that's how it is, I do.' I guess my time in the army and all the experiences I'd had left me no patience for this sort of thing. So that was the end of my brief life as a city butcher, and Edna May and I finally headed for Drouin and that offer my old boss Mr Winters had left open for me all this time: to go into partnership with his old assistant.

Dad was keen for me to do it — he'd still been helping out at the Drouin butcher shop in hopes I'd return and go into the business. So I did. I borrowed the £300 I needed from the Returned Servicemen's League, and that was that. Edna May and I found a house to rent and then eventually we bought one.

But four years of war service would do me few favours back in my home town now. My new partner — whom I won't name because he doesn't deserve a decent one — left all the hard work to me, while he swanned about the shop. He left all the heavy work, all the slaughtering and deliveries to me, and if we had Saturday afternoon slaughtering to do he'd say, 'Yep, I'll meet you at the yards,' and he'd never turn up. And I suspected, as my dad did too, that he was diddling me out of my full share of the profits. He was always splashing money around like he owned the town. I was working harder than I ever had, but was getting nowhere.

Poor Edna May never saw me. She was having to make new friends on her own in a town unfamiliar to her, and sometimes we were that strapped for cash she couldn't even buy herself an ice-cream at the shops. All she did was clean the silly house, listen to the wireless most times for company, and watch me get skinnier while I busted a gut for nothing. I remembered the day, before we got married, that all the girls from Morley's threw her a party, a send-off for her new life with her 'handsome' prince. I wondered if she'd known what she would be in for with this hopeless bushy whether she'd have gone ahead with it.

My outlet was football. I still wasn't very good at it, but, as ever, I was willing. I played mostly with the seconds, a few games with the seniors. I think it was a case of giving the little hero from the war a bit of a go. It was real bush footy. The games were rough and ready and so were the grounds. Out in the Strzeleckis, you would be sliding around in cow manure all afternoon. You would hang your clothes on the fence posts while you played, and come back later to find that horses had been nibbling at them! But we had plenty of fun. There was nothing better than the trip home together in a van, singing all the way, then on to the pub for a beer, or maybe two, if I could afford it.

Some days, I played with Alf Ablett, the future father of Geelong superstar Gary, and grandfather of his sons Gary and Nathan, who both played in Geelong's 2007 premiership team. We didn't know at first if Alf was any good, but were glad to have him because we knew that an uncle of his had played in the reserves in the big league for Richmond. That was how it was in bush footy: you would think it was something special to have a league player in your team, or even someone who was related to a league player. But we soon learned about Alf. He was a classic Ablett. He was about sixteen at the time and lived out in the bush somewhere with his family, putting up telegraph poles.

Another of those newspaper shots of me, this time with the kids at Drouin Public School, showing them my footy 'prowess'.

He didn't train, didn't wash much, and only sometimes turned up on match days, never with any gear. When he did show up, there would be a rush to find him a guernsey, and a pair of shorts and boots. We'd ask, 'What are you going to do today, Alf?'

He'd reply, 'Dunno, get a kick if I can.'

When the match began, he would stand in the middle, never run after the ball, never break into a sweat. But if the ball came within ten feet of him, he'd grab it and as often as not kick a goal from the centre. He was that good. The funny thing is that years later when Gary, his son, played for Myrtleford before he was recruited to Geelong, everyone said he played exactly the same way: he would hardly break into a trot, rarely go far from the centre circle, but dominate the game anyway!

As for me and my ambitions, I had a strange dream one night, a very vivid one: I had some land of my own and I was planting potatoes. It was a dream that stuck with me, and I decided, after six years getting nowhere in Drouin, that's what we'd do: plant potatoes. A bloke offered to sell me some land near Warragul about five miles from Drouin. It wasn't exactly a sheep station: twenty-five acres, with a rickety old house on it, hessian bags over the bathroom windows and rats everywhere. You get the idea. But I thought I could make something of it, so I decided I'd sell up in Drouin and have a go.

Just before I left Drouin, I learned something that made my blood run cold and makes me wonder still to this day. My 'partner' in the butcher's shop said to me, 'You know you've been under surveillance for six years?' I had no idea. I'd brought back with me from Yugoslavia that cap given to me by one of the Partisans, Puks Boris, with whom I'd struck up a friendship. I treasured it and proudly showed it to everyone at the RSL club. Puks also wrote me a number of letters — I think he was still keen on trying to find a way to immigrate to Australia, but he was also just writing because we'd shared an experience — and I showed those around, too. It was all about as innocent as you can get. But this was at the time when McCarthyism was at its peak in the US, and anti-communist sentiment was running high everywhere in the West and the Partisans were communists. It didn't appear to matter to the powers that were in Australia that the Partisans had fought on the side of the Allies in the war, and had been crucial in helping POWs, including me, make it to safety. Nor did it seem to matter that I'd been decorated for my part in the war. No. 'Communist' was a dirty word, the Partisans were communists, I had been with them and was still in touch with one, and so I was a suspicious character.

The weird thing was that everyone was in on the plot, and no-one told me. All the pillars of the town of Drouin: my partner, some in the fire-brigade, the postmaster, the stationmaster, the scoutmaster, the president of the local council, all the bureaucrats at the town hall. Apparently, they were to report if I behaved oddly, or went on strike, or … I don't know, broke into a rendition of the 'Internationale'? I still scratch my head thinking about it. It rattled me so much I never wrote back to Puks again. That's what bloody-minded paranoia does: it can make you paranoid, too.

I was so upset by everything that had been going on in Drouin, I didn't need to be there a second longer; neither did my wife. I suggested to my partner that he take three weeks' leave. When he asked why, I said that I would be gone by then, and I didn't particularly want to see him in the meantime. He said, 'What about the balance of the money you're owed?'

That was, oddly enough, about £300. I replied, 'You can stick it where you like. I'm off.' I'd write off what he owed me and put it down to a lesson learned. I'd made a good profit on the sale of our house anyway. I didn't need his bloody money; just another handful of all he'd no doubt pinched off me anyway.

Around this time, from the stress I suppose, one night I had one of the worst nightmares I've ever had. I thought I was still in the sangers with a mate of mine, my old sergeant Jack Reardon, who was killed at Tobruk. 'Look out, Jack,' I was yelling out. 'Look out.' It wasn't a flashback to a real event, or anything like that, but a mad mix of images and fear and adrenalin.

I woke up to the sounds of Edna May crying, 'Stop!' Or trying to. I had my wife by the throat and I was nearly throttling her. She understood what had gone on; probably better than I did, in a way. She knew I had trouble getting to sleep sometimes, or woke up at odd hours of the night. Usually when that happened it would be a real memory churning through my mind — I was crossing the Drava again, or getting under the apron wire on the Croatian border — anxiety attacks or something like that, I suppose. But this time, I'd hurt my wife. Last of the last straws, that was. I had to move on, in every way.

19
MAKING PEACE

Warragul was meant to be another fresh start for Edna May and me, and in many ways it was. We had a bit of fun fixing up that old house on the farm, or trying to on our limited budget of nil. It was quite a grand old thing, called Carrington: twelve-foot-high ceilings and incredible plaster work round the cornices and ceilings. It sat on a hill overlooking the Latrobe Valley and we could see to the Strzeleckis and the snow on the distant mountains in winter. Priceless view — but with the winds to match.

Then, after a very long wait of almost seven years, my Edna May became, to use the polite term of the times, 'in the family way'. Our daughter, Gayle Nanette, was born at Warragul Hospital on June 10, 1952. If I was jumping out of my skin eight years ago, on June 10, 1944, as that plane came in to pick us up from Bosnia, I was somewhere over the moon this day in '52. Edna May was so thrilled you could have lit a city off the sparkle in her eyes, and our baby, our daughter, was the sweetest, most beautiful thing I'd ever seen. And I — me — I was her father! I was thirty-two. Ernie Brough, a husband, a father, and a potato farmer, and I loved it all.

Nevertheless, my work was back-breaking — I sowed by horse and plough and dug those spuds up by hand with my pitchfork. Edna's dad had come to help me start off, but as much as I loved it, it would never be anything but hard-going. Looking back, I think flogging myself physically on the farm was necessary: it meant I was too busy during the day to think, and too tired at night to do anything but pass out.

But after about five years of it, it was there at Warragul that I reached my lowest ebb. It started the day I came home from the football in town to find that my horse, Bluey, was dying. He was still walking around, but had saliva all around his mouth and looked terrible. Soon afterwards, he was gone. I'd also been having trouble with the potato crop that year; it was just not making enough money to pay the mortgage, let alone provide properly for my family. Then one day, soon after my horse died, I'd dug six bags' worth of potatoes and left them lying in a paddock, near a road. When I came back the next morning, three of the bags were gone. Half my livelihood stolen, just like that. I didn't deserve this: in good times, I'd always give a bag of spuds to whoever called in, even though Edna May would go crook at me. I figured generosity always came back round to the giver. Not this time. I was so angry, I left some bags of potatoes out again the next night, grabbed my old .303, put on my army overcoat and set off to wait for the thieves to come back. Edna May cried, 'You're not going to kill them, are you?' No, I wasn't going to kill them: just scare the shit out of them. I lay out there all night in the rain, itching to send a bullet cracking past the thief's head, but the only creatures I met were a couple of sheep, one of which coughed dismissively at me. I'd never find out who stole my potatoes.

Then, to top it off, a few days after I lost the potatoes, my beagle hound, Tex, got away from me, probably off after a scent. Unknown to me, the bloke next door had laid down poison for the foxes. All that night, I heard thumping noises under our house, and next day found that my dog was there dead. He'd eaten the poison.

So I'd lost my horse, my dog and some of my potatoes. The weeds in my land seemed to be growing faster than anything else, and I still owed a heap of money on the place. I was working myself into the ground so hard I didn't have time to think. And now, it all swamped me. Memories of the war, of being on the run, ran around in my head. I guess they would say now that I was suffering from post-traumatic stress syndrome. Then, there was no such diagnosis, no-one to diagnose it anyway, and no-one to talk to about it. I probably wouldn't have talked to anyone anyway; it just wasn't the way of things then.

Everything seemed so hopeless; I was in a fight I couldn't win. So, one night, I got out my old .303 again, put a bullet in the breach and walked out onto the veranda with every intention of blowing my head off. I sat there for a long time, turning everything over in my mind. The gun was between my legs, its safety catch off. One shot would fix everything, I thought. Eventually, I did fire a shot. But I'd come to my senses — just. I fired over my shoulder and into the roof, deliberately. I felt the discharge, a cracker of crackers, right past my ear. It was that close.

What stopped me? Simple, really: my life was worth more than this. Of course I couldn't do such a thing to my wife, my parents, my daughter. Gayle Nanette was only a toddler at the time. She'd recently got into a pile of cherries Edna May had left by the back door for the second-to-none preserves she'd make from them, and the sight of my little girl, with cherry juice and pulp smeared all over her face — well, how could I rob myself of ever seeing things like that again? Or of seeing my Edna May being followed about by the little poddy lambs we were looking after, or her face the day she killed a tiger snake and chopped it to pieces with a shovel — only to find that by the time I got there, the kookaburras had already pinched the flesh for their supper? Of seeing our little hen adopt some duck eggs, then squawk cranky as hell when her 'chicks' went for a swim in a puddle. I laughed so hard at that! How could I not want to be alive?

I pulled myself together after that night on the veranda, steered clear of the pub to make sure I stayed that way, and got on with the business of living. About a year or so later, after a bumper crop of spuds and peas, I sold the farm for a tidy little profit and went back to butchering, setting up my own shop. Edna May would eventually get that brand-new house she longed for, with a war service loan I took out, and many of those I'd given away bags of spuds to became loyal customers. As they say, what goes around does come around, given time. Generosity is never a silly idea.

Edna May and I would never be too flush for cash, but we were never poor again either. My left hand would still shake like mad whenever I got keyed up about something, but it became a reminder that whatever life threw at me I'd always know that I'd survived worse.

20
TAKE IT FROM AN OLD BLOKE

Eric, Allan and I could hardly have been closer to one another if we had been surgically fused during our wartime adventures. We'd bonded, as they say now. We knew each other's minds and hearts. It was the sort of closeness that comes only from confronting death together, again and again. We were close in age, too. Allan was born in 1917 and Eric in 1918, me in 1920. We were more like brothers than companions. But after the war, we scarcely saw one another again. The world then was larger, travel more expensive and less common. People stayed in their own places. We never wrote to each other; we weren't letter-writing sort of people.

Over the years, Allan came to visit me twice, and I went once to Western Australia to see him. It was on a grand bus tour of Australia Edna May and I did in '84, after I retired. Knowing I was a butcher, Allan took me to where he bought his meat, and to the meat market at Fremantle — only a good mate who knows what you're about would think to do that sort of thing. He'd married and had three daughters and a boy, called Allan too. He'd spent his working life on the trams. We had a great time together those couple of days we spent in Fremantle. Neither of us knew that would be the very last time we'd meet.

It wasn't until 1990, when I was seventy, that I finally rang Eric in New Zealand and said: 'You'd better get the horse and jinker out. I'm coming over.' It was forty-six years since we'd parted that day in Italy. Eric had retired from his business as a fencing contractor, and lived with his wife in Wanganui, a town on the North Island. He'd never had kids of his own, but he had made many friends, and he called upon a good many of them across both the North and South Islands and took us on a grand tour of the whole country. A couple of years later, Eric came to Melbourne and we took him on a tour. It was slightly less grand, but we still had a terrific time. I was retired, too, by then, of course, but still worked part time cutting lawns and doing odd handyman jobs — I was always working at something! — and Eric cheerfully joined in.

What was most remarkable about these meetings with Eric and Allan is that we found we still thought the same way after so many years had passed. It was as if the telepathy we had developed while we were on the run in wartime Europe had remained intact. Then, we had barely ever needed to talk to know what to do next. One would think of something, and the next minute we would all do it together. It's like sheep when they run: one does, then they all do. Decades later, it was the same. Eric and I would be out driving, and he would say, 'Look at the design of that house. It's all wrong.' Or, 'Looks like rain, we'd better take our coats.' Whatever it was he said, I would have been thinking the same thing at the same moment, his words like an echo, and vice versa. It happened time and time again.

Allan died suddenly in 1985, aged sixty-seven, not long after the last time we met. He didn't look or seem crook at the time, but as his daughter said, he never properly recovered from the privations he suffered during the war. Eric died in 1999, just short of his eighty-first birthday. I'm the only survivor now.

~

Gradually, throughout the late 1990s, Edna May started to show signs that she had dementia. I had to give up my part-time lawn-mowing to look after her — it was probably about time, anyway, since I was eighty-three. Then one day at home, she slipped and fell as she walked around the kitchen table, and could not get up. I called an ambulance. She'd broken her hip. She went to hospital for about six weeks, then to a nursing home. It was a rotten time, to say the least. I would go out to see her and feed her every day, and our daughter did the same in the evenings. We brought Edna May home for a time, but she hurt her hip again and ended up back in hospital, and then back in the nursing home permanently. It was dreadful. I felt so very helpless, on my wife's behalf.

I know that when my time comes, I won't go into a home; they're horrible places. My daughter says to me, 'You'll need me when you get old.' I always say, 'No I won't. I'll go down to Lorne and jump off a cliff.' I wouldn't put up with the indignity.

My Edna May died on June 27, 2004. She was not quite eighty-two. My treasured keepsake to remind me of her is her little cat, Sandy. She's a golden-ginger cat with white paws and tummy, and a very elegant white tip on her tail. She's become my household companion. She sleeps at the end of my bed and gets up every morning at six o'clock on the knocker. She disappears for an hour and a half, comes in for a feed, then minds her own business for the rest of the day. She's the boss and a lady — she only enters via the front door, of course. She comes inside in the evening for a feed. When she hears the music at the end of the *7.30 Report* on the ABC, she comes into the lounge, then leads me off to bed. We've become a bit of an odd couple. I look after her diet and she gives me reproving looks if I'm late with her meals, or to get me to go to bed.

It's been lonely since my wife died, but I'm grateful for the cat and the purring noises she makes at night. I mustn't have too many nightmares these days because Sandy never moves from her spot on the bed, and she's always there in the morning. The rhythm of her breathing and purring is a comfort to me. I don't know what I'd do if she died now. Maybe jump off that cliff!

~

I didn't really talk about the war much until recently. For a long time, no-one wanted to listen; it wasn't fashionable. Now, fortunately, lots of people are curious about where we went, how we fought and what we endured during those years. Anzac Day has become a really big thing. I guess we Diggers are getting old and our numbers are thinning, and the younger generations feel a need to know.

A little while ago, I presented a Rats of Tobruk flag to the high school just down the road from me in Belmont and gave a little talk to the kids. The principal was eager to know more and I was happy to oblige him. I'm glad of the chance to talk and reflect now. It's a good way, probably the best way, to help get the war experiences out of your system, out of the lonely silence of your head and into the open. But it's taken a long, long time for me to get to this point. As I've said, we didn't have any counselling or psychological therapies to help us, as they have today.

But even for today's returning soldiers, coming back from Iraq or Afghanistan, it would be a hard road — the same road, the same anxiety and nightmares and shakes and grogging on to overcome. And I'm sure plenty of men today, as in my day, don't seek help when they most need it. I'm sure the military authorities could do a lot more to help in that regard, too, if only they thought about it.

I'm lucky that I still enjoy good health. I've always kept myself occupied, and I think that's part of the secret to a long life. I saw a slogan in a clinic once that I think sums up my attitude: 'Plan to live, don't plan to die.' I haven't made a will. To me, that would be like signing my own death warrant. I eat healthy food, make a fine stir-fry, if I do say so myself, and I rarely drink. I'm still active: I grow citrus fruits and Cypress cuttings in my backyard and do odd jobs for friends, lawn-mowing and weed-spraying, for instance. I don't take money for it now because I don't need it these days.

I live alone, but my daughter and two granddaughters ring me or call in regularly; so do my friends. The local branch of the Rats of Tobruk has disbanded — we ran out of numbers for a quorum — but I still go to the RSL club regularly and have good friends there, too. My best mate in my later years was a millionaire. He was a shy bloke and told me he didn't want his name in any book, so I can't name him, even though he passed away last year. Despite his millions he remained a simple, decent man, and a great friend. Once, when I didn't answer the phone one day, he came all the way down to my house just to make sure I was all right. One way or another, I've been lucky to have people looking out for me all my life.

~

One night in the middle of 2006, I was watching television when an item was screened about new developments in stem cell research coming out of St Vincent's Hospital in Melbourne, and how much good it might do to cure and prevent disease. I thought it sounded like a really worthwhile project. A little while previously, I'd sold some land I'd bought cheaply at nearby Moriac. With all the improvements I'd made to the land over the years, it ended up fetching the princely sum of $640,000. I gave a big chunk of it to my daughter, and some to my granddaughters, but I still had more than I needed. I live a pretty simple lifestyle and, besides, it is not as if I can take it with me.

I was inspired by what I had learned about stem cell research, but I didn't know how to get in touch with anyone in medical research to offer a donation. The only number I had was an emergency dementia number that was still pinned to the wall from when my wife was ill. So I rang it. 'What's your problem?' the woman asked. She probably thought I was going off my head. Maybe I was.

I explained that I needed a number for St Vincent's. I was put through. The next thing I knew, a lady called Vivienne Talbot from the hospital was visiting me. She was very thorough. She wanted to make sure that I wasn't giving away money I needed. I assured her I was fine. Then she said that the stem cell project, though certainly worthy, got funds from the government or somewhere else. St Vincent's had an urgent need — but not enough money — for another piece of medical equipment. It was called an echocardiography machine. It provided three-dimensional images of the heart, making it easier to detect abnormalities and plan treatment. It sounded like an eminently worthy cause, so I gave St Vincent's $300,000.

When the machine arrived, I was given a demonstration. I could see the blood flowing from one valve to another. On the side, there was a kind of speedo that told you how much blood was being pumped at any one time, and how quickly. Before long, they said the machine had found a vein that no-one had seen before. It was fascinating. Dr Andrew MacIsaac, director of the coronary care unit at the hospital, offered to have a look at my heart with the machine when it arrived. 'No. You won't find anything there,' I said. 'Just a big stone!'

St Vincent's made a bit of a fuss of me when the machine was installed. They sent a taxi to Geelong to pick me up, gave me a tour of the heart unit and took me out to lunch in Carlton. Mind you, Vivienne got her money's worth — she came down and raided my lemon tree!

On Anzac Day the next year, the story appeared on the front page of *The Age*, written by the journalist Greg Baum, complete with a picture of me sitting on a box outside my old garage. The headline read: 'The Digger who gave his all, plus another $300,000 to boot.' That was a very nice article to read first thing on Anzac Day, and then I got on the train at Geelong station for the march. That afternoon, I went for a drink with my mates at Tobruk House in Melbourne — and won the raffle! As I've said often, for a bloke who could have died many times, I've lived a lucky life.

Best of all, just a couple of weeks ago, Dr McIsaac finally got me on his precious echocardiography machine and proved me wrong: I do, indeed, have a heart, and a pretty strong one, too.

~

War's a damnable thing. Don't let anyone ever tell you otherwise. The damage runs deep. All those nights for decades afterwards I would lie in bed thinking, I've got to get under the wire tonight. Gotta get under the wire tonight. Or gotta make it to the riverbank. My mate Henry Pegrum reckons it's like a gramophone stuck in the groove, going round and round, stuck on a memory. It's true, but they are more like pictures for me now, impressed in my memory, chapters inside my whole life, and they don't upset me any more.

It's hard for people to get an idea of how it is for soldiers on the front line. When you see them on the television, you might think that because they're out on patrol together, carrying rifles, they feel in control. But it's not like that. All the time, they will be waiting for someone to open up on them. They will be waiting for the world to explode. They will know that danger is all around, and it will play on their minds. It did on ours. Constant tension and, yes, fear — even if you don't admit it to yourself at the time. Maybe because I was young enough and stupid enough, I learned to suppress my fear — and the army drilled that into us. You had to suppress fear and go with the adrenalin to survive, let alone do your job. But that doesn't mean my brain wasn't registering it.

Most soldiers will bring the war home with them in some form. Some will never forget it; some will die from it, from suicide or alcoholism, years after the guns have packed up and gone home. You see, it's just not natural for human beings to go out and kill other humans. And that's what war's all about. That's what the army is about in a time of war. You're standing there at training with a rifle and bayonet, and someone says, 'Go, go on. Stick him in the guts.' It's only a bale of hay, suspended from a frame. But in your mind it's a person. Before you're even on the front line, it's brutalising. Some blokes are just about spewing when they get to the hay bale. Others don't even make it; they faint and fall over thinking about it. It's funny, seeing strapping big blokes waiting in a queue to see the doctor with his needles and sedatives later. But it's not really funny at all.

I didn't ever knowingly kill an enemy soldier. Almost all the fighting I did was at night, and none of it was hand-to-hand. I fired bullets into the dark and dodged the bullets coming back. I have no way of knowing what the bullets I fired did. No way of knowing what happened after I threw that one grenade at El Alamein. It is all so random anyway. But that didn't make it any easier. I've often wondered how I would have fared if it had come to a point where I had to deliberately shoot at another human being, even if it was in self-defence. I can't say for sure what I would have done. While I was with the Partisans, they were planning one night to execute a prisoner, and the poor, wretched man looked at me with pleading eyes, silently begging for me to try to spare him. But if I'd kicked up a fuss, the next bullet would have been for me. I had to look away but his face haunts me still.

War is just idiotic. Think of a tank. All that fine steel. All that work. All that technology and intricate design. Those machine guns, operating perfectly. Probably worth half a million dollars. Then a shell hits it, sets it alight and it's gone.

The shell cost, what, $600, $700? Make sense of that. It's just such a comprehensive waste.

A bloke said something to me last year that I liked: 'If all the politicians, and all the men over the age of forty were sent to war instead of the army,' he said, 'there wouldn't be a war. They'd sit down, have a beer and find another way.'

Of course, there are psychopaths who won't learn any other way. I know. I went to fight one: Hitler. A tyrant who uses the armed forces to torture and kill even his own people won't listen to reason. So there will always be war. And it will never be anything other than horrendous folly. Death and destruction.

We humans are capable of so much better than that. Across the world and all languages and all religions, it would be the rarest thing to find a soul who doesn't know what the goodness in life is. It's generosity, kindness, compassion, sharing. It's about that phone call to a friend just to say hello. It's about doing that favour for someone you don't have to do. Just the other day I cut some corn for my good friend Margaret in Geelong, a neighbour whose husband recently passed away, and when I lugged that basket of corn inside for her, she gave me some lovely soup to take home. That's goodness. It doesn't cost you anything, everyone wins, and it's so easy. It's what I like to call 'heaven on earth', and if this old bloke has one piece of advice to impart it's this: Live your heaven on earth — today.

ACKNOWLEDGEMENTS

I'd like to say thank you to the following people:

My parents, Ernest and Anne Brough, my granddaughter Sally Anne Cooper, and my sister Marjorie Harrison, as well as Greg Baum, Dr MacIsaac, Kim Swivel, Fiona Henderson, Shirley Walsh, Phillip Jones, Winifred Doyle, Clare Forster, Liz Campbell, and all those who've assisted me at St Vincent's Hospital, Melbourne, and HarperCollins in Sydney. Without you and your help, my story would not have made it out of my memories and onto these pages.

Finally, I would like to single out the two people who brought my adventures onto these pages.

Journalist Greg Baum wrote a story about me that ran on the front page of *The Age* on Anzac Day 2007. Greg's story and his subsequent interviews with me were the seeds from which this book grew. After many further chats, writer and editor Kim Swivel did a fine job of weeding and pruning all my words along the way.

Greg Baum has been a journalist for thirty years, the last twenty with the Melbourne *Age*. His work has also appeared in the London *Guardian, Wisden Cricket Almanack* and on ABC radio. He has won many sports-writing awards and a Walkley for his journalism. He lives in Melbourne.

Kim Swivel is an editor and writer. Her first novel, *Black Diamonds*, was published in 2007, under the name Kim Kelly, and she is working on her second. She lives in the Blue Mountains.